Broken Beautiful

CHRISSIE MOORE

Broken Beautiful

ISBN: 979-8-9989009-0-7
First Edition

Edited by Missing Piece Virtual Solutions and Sherry Jones

Book design by Missing Piece Virtual Solutions

Back Cover Photo Credit to Liam Grayson Shehi

This is a work of nonfiction. Names and identifying details may have been changed to protect the privacy of individuals. The views and opinions expressed are those of the author and do not necessarily reflect those of the publisher.

Printed in the United States of America

For permissions, inquiries, or more information, please contact the author directly.

Forward: By Paul Ybarra

I still remember the day I met Chrissie. I can't recall the exact season, but the moment itself is unforgettable. We crossed paths in the hallway at church, and our conversation quickly turned to an unexpected request: *"Can you give my son a job?"* Little did I know that this simple exchange would spark a journey—one that would inspire me to look deeper into myself as the years went by.

I watched Chrissie transition from one season of life to another, each step refining her in ways neither of us could have anticipated. I vividly recall the moment she first heard about our ministry. As I explained its purpose, I sensed a quiet resistance, an unspoken sentiment that echoed, *"I don't need that."*

Not in those exact words, but the undercurrent was there. Yet, something stirred within her. The following week, she walked through the doors, not realizing that what she thought was for her family and children was, in fact, for *her*.

God had orchestrated a divine appointment, drawing her into a process of transformation. She went from hiding behind a smile to confronting the true enemy of her soul, stepping into the authority that had been hers all along. She pushed past the pain of her past and embraced the fullness of God's plan for her life.

Chrissie, I am so incredibly proud of you. Your perseverance, your courage, and the way you have allowed God to shape you into the beautiful, redeemed woman you are today is nothing short of remarkable. My prayer is that your journey will inspire and transform the lives of many women, equipping them to walk in their own freedom and purpose.

Much love to you, my friend!

Paul
#brokenbeautiful

This book is dedicated to several people~

To my mom Petra- She lived in abuse for over 25 years and pushed through the pain and survived. I saw her fight daily to keep her joy. I saw her learn and love again even when she was up against every statistic. She's gone home to be with the Lord, but she will forever be my hero.

To my sister Cyndee~ You have been in my corner since we were kids. I couldn't have done anything without your love and support. I love you every day of my life. You are my best friend.

To Jess~ You are and will always be my "*WHY*". Your courage is beautiful. Let your heart always remain tender to God's voice. May your journey be filled with joy, laughter and beautiful memories. You chose to live in God's truth not your trauma. May your story change many women's lives.

To Paul & Hollie Ybarra~ You walked alongside me through the roughest parts of my life. I was a tough nut to crack but it never stopped you both from loving me. I am so grateful for your friendship, prayers and nights by the fire. I cherish these memories always.

To my children Justin, Josh, Jeremy & Jess~ We have fought so hard to be where we are today and there is still so much to learn. May the God who saved each of you, continue to use your individual story for HIS GLORY. I love you more than words can ever express.

To the person God used to help me feel again~ Thank you for your *friendship.* I don't think you'll ever understand what it's like to no longer be numb.

To EVERY SINGLE WOMAN God put in my path~

Who prayed with me and for me, who cheered me on, listened to my story, cried with me, laughed with me, loved me in my mess and encouraged me to finish this book. I love and honor you all. There are too many to name, but I remember every single encounter. I went silent so many times because my pain was too great, but YOU NEVER stopped loving or believing in me. And lastly, to every woman who suffered in silence, feels unseen and may still be enduring abuse. I pray my story empowers you to reclaim your voice.

Table of Contents

Chapters:

Introduction:

As little girls, we grow up dreaming of a fairytale life. A world where everything is perfect, beautiful and we live happily ever after. Abuse was never a part of my dreams. Victims of abuse often don't realize the severity of pain they are hiding behind until they have been removed from their abuser or abusive environment.

Abuse has different tentacles, and they can each damage differently. Whether its psychological, mental, emotional, verbal, or sexual abuse, each one leaves deep wounds and are often not identified until many years later. Counselors call it Post Traumatic Stress Disorder or PTSD. They call it that because at the time of the traumatic events, we are not confronting the abuse but rather living in survival mode.

Although I am not a counselor or a therapist, I can speak from experience. I learned to hide my pain and function in the chaos of fear, control and manipulation. I am a survivor of mental, verbal, psychological and sexual abuse. No one knew I was being abused. Not all abuse is visible.

I fell in love with a man who showed no signs of abusive behavior. From the outside, we had the perfect family. We had a big house, a nice car, and a manicured lawn in a pretty little neighborhood. We attended PTA meetings, sporting events and volunteered every opportunity we had. We were the typical All American "Perfect Family".

My single friends would tell me how lucky I was to have such a kind, handsome and helpful husband. He was charming, funny, and always willing to help anyone at any time. He loved being the center of attention. What no one knew was he had a secret life. It was a side to him that I did not know existed until many years into our marriage.

The man people would see wasn't the man I saw behind closed doors. He made sexual comments to my close friends and played it off as a joke. He was on Pornographic Chat rooms and swingers' sites. He constantly looked for attention from women and though he got all the attention he wanted; it was never enough. His sexual appetite grew to an uncontrollable proportion, until it eventually destroyed him. The destruction he left behind is something we still are healing from today nearly 12 years later.

I want every woman who has experienced abuse to know that you are not alone. We are Drs., Lawyers, Nurses, Teachers, pastor's wives, stay at home moms, sisters and friends. As you read my story, I pray that God will set you free from fear, guilt, shame and rejection. You are beautiful. You were always enough.

Chapter 1
The Invisible Threads of Generational Trauma

Generational trauma, also known as transgenerational trauma or intergenerational trauma, refers to the psychological and emotional wounds passed down from one generation to the next (Mark Wolynn https://markwoylnn.com/it-didnt-start-with-you/)

Growing up, life was anything but easy. I was raised in a home filled with violence. Some of my earliest memories, at just six years old, are of hiding– curled up in my closet or tucked beneath my bed. Those small, dark spaces became my refuge on the nights my father unleashed his rage on my mother.

My mother married my father when she was young, though she often spoke about how she never truly wanted to. She described it as an arranged marriage—one she had no choice but to accept. She told me how, one day, she came home from work to find my father sitting in her living room, deep in conversation with my grandfather. Without her knowledge, plans were already in motion.

He was going to ask her out, and her family, familiar with his grandmother from across the street, had already welcomed the idea. She was never drawn to him—not in the slightest. So when he showed up at her house, uninvited and already making plans, she felt uneasy.

My mother was beautiful—her olive skin and striking hazel eyes made her impossible to overlook. Her smile could light up an entire room. But despite her beauty, she was quiet and reserved, spending most of her time focused on school and work. She didn't have many friends, and the money she earned went straight to helping her family. She once told me about a boy from school she had truly loved.

Whenever she spoke of him, her face would light up, her voice filled with excitement. But she never explained why they never ended up together. That love, that spark—none of it existed between her and my father. She went out with him not because she wanted to, but because she felt she had no choice.

Defying my grandparents wasn't something she could imagine doing, so, against her own heart's wishes, she went along with it. When he took her out, he drove to a secluded spot and parked the car. My mom said a lump formed in her throat as fear crept in—she could already sense his intentions.

At first, he made small talk, but it didn't take long before he got to the point. He told her he had already decided they were going to get married. Then, leaning in closer, he said, *"Since we're going to be husband and wife, we might as well have sex"*.

When my mom was around 16, she had heard her friends talking about sex, but she didn't fully understand what it meant. Curious, she asked my grandmother about it. Instead of an answer, she received a slap across the face. *"Never speak of that again,"* my grandmother warned. *"And if I ever find out you're doing it, you'll be in big trouble."*

That moment stayed with her. So, when he started pressuring her, they were going to be married anyway, fear and panic took over. She didn't want to marry him. She didn't want to give in to him. But with each attempt to resist, the knot in her stomach tightened until she felt like she might vomit. After several failed attempts to pressure her, my dad grew frustrated. He told her that if she didn't give in, his erection wouldn't go away unless he went to the hospital for a shot. Confused and scared, my mom asked *"What kind, of shot?" "The kind that makes it go down,"* he responded. Then, his tone darkened *"If you don't do this with me, everyone will know you aroused me—which means you wanted it. And if they find out, your parents will be upset and never speak to you again."*

My mom felt trapped. The slap from my grandmother all those years ago had already taught her—this wasn't something she could talk about. She didn't want to disappoint her parents, and the fear of being disowned terrified her. She felt trapped, and she reluctantly gave in. She told me how she cried through it, feeling nothing but shame, anger, and disgust.

There was no love, no connection—just a deep sense of violation. When he dropped her off that night, she was so overwhelmed with fear and regret that she ran inside and threw up. How was she ever going to escape this? A month later, she realized she was pregnant —with me. As she shared this painful memory, tears welled in her eyes. She looked at me and said, "You were sent to save me."

I didn't understand what she meant at the time, but years later, I had the privilege of leading her to the Lord—a moment that brought her the peace she had long searched for. She explained that her timid nature made her an easy target, and my dad picked up on that immediately. He knew she wouldn't need much persuading to bend to his will.

Over the years, he groomed her—planting seeds of doubt, breaking down her confidence, and making her believe she was nothing without him. He threatened her life, her family's lives, and her future. *"You'll never be anything,"* he would say. *"You're not smart enough to survive without me."* She endured the verbal assaults, the relentless beatings—night after night, year after year. And when the chance to escape finally came, she couldn't leave.

Not because she didn't want to, but because fear had paralyzed her. My dad had conditioned her to believe that leaving wasn't an option. His threats weren't just words—they were promises. And he made sure she knew exactly where she belonged. My mom had no idea my dad was an alcoholic when she married him. It wasn't until years later that she learned about his past—how his mother had abandoned him and left him to be raised by his grandmother.

Back then, harsh beatings were called discipline, not abuse. As my dad grew older, he turned to alcohol to dull the pain. But drinking only fueled his anger, and with that anger came violence. I often wondered if, when he lashed out at my mom, he was really fighting demons from his past.

Since she couldn't defend herself, it was too easy for him to take his rage out on her. While my mom was pregnant with me, my dad beat her relentlessly, hoping she would miscarry.

When that didn't work, he took her to Reynosa, Mexico, for a so-called "shot" that was supposed to terminate the pregnancy. He brought her there three times, but it never worked. God had other plans for me. I always knew my dad never wanted children—he made that painfully clear. But learning just how far he was willing to go to prevent my birth left me carrying the weight of rejection throughout my life. Looking back,

I can see God's love and protection over me, even before I was born. Still, abuse was woven into my family's history long before I ever entered this world. Growing up, I craved approval—especially from men. I felt like I constantly had to prove my worth, as if I was never enough. I hated being home because of the abuse I witnessed.

I longed for something—anything—to numb the pain. All I wanted was for my mom's screams to stop. Covering my ears and hiding in my closet didn't drown out the noise. I felt alone. Afraid. My closet became my refuge, the only place where I felt safe. It was long and narrow, and I would retreat to the very back, where piles of dirty clothes usually sat.

I would push them aside, clearing a small space in the middle, then bury myself beneath them. The smell was awful, but I didn't care. The scent of dirty laundry was nothing compared to the fear outside that door. In that hidden corner, I felt invisible. No one could see me. No one could find me. No one could hurt me. When I turned 16, I found a different way to numb my pain—I started partying and smoking weed. It helped take the edge off because home was anything but a refuge. Every time I walked up the driveway, I felt the knot in my stomach tighten. Would he be awake? Would there be yelling? Would he call me a whore or spit out some other cruel insult?

After a big fight, I could usually hear my mom crying in her room. I would lie on the floor, looking under my bedroom door to see if it was safe to come out.

My breathing was heavy, but I tried to be as quiet as I could. I was terrified that if I breathed too loudly, he would hear me. My heart pounded so hard I thought it might give me away. As I laid there, I begged God to rescue my mom. To get us out of this hell we called home. After what felt like an eternity,

I finally heard my dad's footsteps—slow, almost hesitant, as if he felt some regret for what he had done. Step by step, he moved away, always mumbling to himself but I never knew what he said. Then I heard the back screen door slam shut behind him. He was outside now. I could finally take a breath. It was over—for now, at least.

The house fell into an eerie silence. The only sound was the faint whimpers coming from my parents' room. She was trying to be quiet, but I could hear her pain. —The house felt heavy, like a thick fog. It pressed down on me, paralyzing me, swallowing me whole. I knew that my mom must have felt the same thing. I stood up quietly, trying to not make a lot of noise. I turned around and behind me was my sister Cyndee curled up in the corner, rocking back and forth.

It was the only way she knew how to cope. Sometimes she would hum, other times she would sing softly—always the same melody, though I never knew what it was. It was her way of drowning out the violence, night after night. Gently, I reached for the door, pushing it open just enough to peek outside. The hinges let out a sharp screech, making my heart race. I knew my mom would hear me. *"Chris, go back to your room,"* she whispered, *"I'm okay, but I need a minute."* She wasn't okay. I could hear the sadness in her voice.

I knew she was trying to be strong, but it was evident she was in so much pain. Every part of me wanted to run to her, hold her, but I knew she needed to be alone. I was only nine years old, but I made myself a promise that night. I would never marry a man like my father.

I quietly slipped back into my room, where my sister was still rocking back and forth. I touched her on the shoulder and said, *"Mom is ok for now, let's try to get some sleep."* Cyndee looked up and slowly crawled into bed. She still looked disassociated with what just happened.

I laid down and focused on the fan moving back and forth until exhaustion put me to sleep. I begged for a miracle. But the miracle never came. At the time, I didn't realize that my mom had been groomed to fear my dad. And without knowing it, my sister and I were groomed to believe that staying in an abusive marriage was normal—even expected.

My mom stayed because, growing up Catholic, she had been taught that marriage was sacred in the eyes of the Lord. No matter how much she suffered, she believed it was a wife's duty to stand by her husband. She loved God, but she often questioned why He would want a woman to remain in an abusive marriage.

Ignorance can be passed down from generation to generation, and when it is, the cycle of abuse continues—unquestioned and tolerated. She stayed because she believed it was the right thing to do for her children. Divorce was shameful, a disgrace that left women ostracized. What played over and over in her mind were the constant threats my dad made- *"Where would you go?" "How could you survive without me?" "Who would want you after having kids?"* He knew exactly how to make her feel invisible, unworthy of love.

He knew the words that would keep her silent, trapped in fear. And over time, she believed them. He also threatened that if she left, he would find her, kill her, and then murder her parents and younger brother—the person she loved most. To her, the threats were real. She couldn't risk escaping, only to be caught and beaten even worse. So, she stayed. Her voice was silenced, her confidence crushed. She learned to keep her head down and her mouth shut. Over time, she was groomed to believe she didn't deserve happiness—that this was her fate, her punishment. *For better or worse, till death do they part.*

Most of the time, we hid in our room. When I wasn't home, I numbed the pain with drinking and drugs.

However, when I was home, I needed another way to cope. Fear and anxiety consumed me. I didn't know how to make it stop, so I cleaned—obsessively.

I thought that if I made my room spotless, if everything was in perfect order, maybe my dad would stop hitting my mom. Maybe he would love me. With every scream, I scrubbed harder, folded faster, desperate to control something... anything. But no matter how clean my room was, the violence never stopped.

My sister had her own way of coping. She would rock herself back and forth on the floor, shutting out the world until she was completely zoned out. She wouldn't snap out of it until I whispered that the fight was over. Then, as if waking out of a trance, she would come back to reality. Most of the time she still sat there numb. Even as a child, I felt an emptiness inside me—something was missing, but I couldn't name it.

The void was consuming. I felt invisible, even in a room full of people. More than anything, I wanted to be seen, to be loved, to have someone recognize that I was a good person. I ached for love, even though I didn't know what it truly was. What I didn't realize at the time was that I was searching for something my father had never given me—his love, his approval, his presence.

But deep down, I knew I would never get it. No matter how hard I tried, nothing I did was ever good enough. So, I convinced myself that if I could just be perfect, maybe then I'd feel whole. But perfection didn't fill the emptiness—it only made it worse.

The first time I had sex, I cried. It wasn't love at all. It wasn't even with someone I cared about. I only did it because my friends said that if I wanted to find love, I had to have a lot of sex and learn to get good at it.

The guy was someone I had known for maybe a few weeks.

I'd heard he liked me, and that seemed like reason enough. But the moment it happened; all I could think about was how dirty I felt. We barely spoke. It was dark, the atmosphere awkward, and it was clear he just wanted to get it over with. I had no idea what I was doing. I just laid there, waiting for some kind of magic, some fireworks that never came. It was supposed to be special; something that made me feel wanted and cherished.

He was supposed to hold me afterward, whispering how much he loved me. But after a few minutes, it was over. He got dressed, casually said he'd see me at school, and walked out. I laid there, staring at the ceiling, trying to make sense of it. *What just happened?* If this was what sex was supposed to be, then it didn't make me feel loved at all.

In fact, it left me feeling even more lost. *"If sex wasn't love, then what was?"* I was desperate to find love, but I had no idea what I was doing. I went out with different guys, drowned myself in drugs and alcohol, trying to numb the pain. But no matter how much I tried to escape; I still woke up every morning feeling empty and alone.

I had lost several friends because they thought I partied too much. The crazy thing is no one ever asked "*WHY*" I drank so much. I wished I had someone to confide in. I never told anyone about the abuse. It was too embarrassing. A few months after losing my virginity, I met someone who felt different. He was kind, fun, and for the first time, I thought I had found real love. He WAS my first love.

Our relationship was built on sex. We cared about each other and even loved spending time together, but deep down, I lived in constant fear that he would leave me. I was needy, insecure, and completely unaware that the rejection I had faced from my father had shaped my idea of love into something unhealthy and desperate. I convinced myself he truly loved me.

I let him control my decisions while he spent his nights out with friends, and even after he cheated, I stayed. As painful as it was, I thought enduring his betrayal was better than facing loneliness.

Over time, our constant physical relationship led to the inevitable—I became pregnant. I was 17. With an abusive father at home, I knew he would never accept it. Out of fear for my mother's safety and my own, I was urged to have an abortion. The emotional and mental weight of everything eventually ended our relationship, leaving me with deep trauma that I knew I had to heal from.

Grooming is a manipulative process used by a predator for the purpose of creating a sense of trust with a targeted person. Thus, before selecting their victims, abusers often scope out and observe possible 'candidates' and select them based on ease of access to them or their perceived vulnerability. Those who have family problems, who lack confidence and self-esteem, or are already abuse survivors. -Psychology today

Marriage was something I had always dreamed of. Like many little girls, I imagined the beautiful wedding, the stunning dress, and a room full of people celebrating love. I had watched *Cinderella* more times than I could count, clinging to the hope that one day, my own Prince Charming would come and rescue me from the life I so badly wanted to escape.

I often disappeared into a dream world—it was the only way I knew how to cope. With a father who was neither a loving husband nor a caring dad, I turned to sitcoms, movies, and books for my idea of love. I lived in a world of fiction, wrapped up in fairy tales that felt far more comforting than reality.

I devoured romance novels, counted down the days until the next sappy movie hit theaters, and convinced myself that someday, my prince would come.

Then, one day, he came into my life. I wasn't searching for anyone. In fact, I had promised myself I didn't want to date anyone for a while. Despite my loyalty, my ex had found someone else and left me behind. My heart was still raw, my wounds too fresh. The last thing I needed was another relationship. I felt like a walking target, vulnerable and exposed.

At the time, I was invited to visit my ex-boyfriend's ex-girlfriend in Arkansas. I know—it sounds ridiculous. But somehow, our shared heartbreak created an unspoken bond. It wasn't the wisest decision, but it gave me an escape, a way to put distance between myself and the pain I had just endured.

We do our best to mask our wounds with forced smiles, blending in as if everything is fine. But in the silence, when no one is watching, the weight of our struggles grows deafening.

Unfortunately, there are always men who can spot the wounded bird—and at that time, I was the wounded bird. No matter how hard I tried to conceal my pain, it was still visible to those who knew how to look.

I was waiting for my friend to finish her class. She had let us borrow her car so we could drive from her house to the school.

Once she was out, we all walked together to the cafeteria. As I looked around, I saw a sea of unfamiliar faces. Groups of students gathered in their usual cliques, talking and laughing, much like my high school, only now I was in a completely different place.

I felt out of my element, nervous and unsettled—especially since I had never traveled outside my hometown, let alone to a state where I was the minority. As we wandered through the cafeteria, searching for a place to sit, a guy passed by me slowly, he smiled at me.

I didn't smile back—I was caught off guard. After we sat down, I noticed him moving through the room, stopping to chat with different people. Something about him lingered in my mind, though I couldn't quite place why. There was something familiar about him, yet we had never met. I wasn't trying to be obvious, but when I turned around to casually glance in his direction, something caught my attention—his boots.

They were the most unique pair of black ostrich pointed-toe cowboy boots I had ever seen. I felt ridiculous staring at them, but I couldn't help myself. Maybe I had watched too many western movies, but for some reason, I couldn't take my eyes off him—or his boots.

I kept reminding myself that I wasn't looking for a relationship. I didn't want to think about men, love, or anything remotely close to it. Yet, despite my best efforts, the longing to be loved was undeniable. It felt like a neon sign flashing above my head, visible to anyone who cared to look.

I didn't want him to think I was staring, but I couldn't seem to stop glancing in his direction. There was something about him that drew people in—his charisma was undeniable. As I got a closer look, I noticed his dirty blond hair, styled in a perfectly feathered mullet. Every now and then, as he spoke to people, he would run his fingers through it, adding to his charm.

He carried himself with such confidence, striking up conversations with everyone around him. I looked away for just a moment to talk to my friend, but when I glanced back, he was gone. Why is my heart racing? My breath quickened, and tiny beads of sweat formed on my forehead.

Where did he go? He was just by the corner table... I scanned the room, trying to spot him, when suddenly—there he was. He appeared right in front of me, as if he had known exactly where he was headed all along. His eyes locked onto mine, and I could feel my throat tighten. I swallowed hard—so hard, I was sure everyone around me heard it. Was it just me, or did the entire cafeteria fade into the background? My heartbeat pounded so loudly, I swore it echoed in my ears.

Have you ever wondered if the people around you can sense your pain? Do they truly notice when we're at our most vulnerable? I believe that when we're deeply wounded, we often fail to see our own unhealthy patterns—patterns that can unintentionally draw in others who are just as broken.

I wanted to move, to do something, but instead, I stood frozen, like a deer caught in headlights. He kept staring at me, and after what felt like an eternity (though, realistically, it was probably only two minutes), he smiled again. But this time, I felt like melted butter on warm pancakes. "Get a grip, Chrissie. What is wrong with you?" I told myself.

I had no idea what else to do, so I simply smiled back. No words were exchanged, yet somehow, it felt as if he could see straight into my thoughts. A whirlwind of thoughts flooded my mind. What does this guy want from me? If he only knew what I had just been through, he wouldn't be looking at me like this.

His attention caught me off guard, and though part of me felt flattered, I wasn't in the right headspace.

I was still carrying the weight of my past relationship, the pain lingering like a shadow. How do I handle this? Should I act uninterested? Play it off like I don't care? Before I could figure it out, he turned and walked away, disappearing into the crowd. A few moments later, his friend approached me with a grin. "Hey, I have a friend named Chris—he's standing over there—and he wants to know if he can take you out on a date. What do you think?"

My first thought was, *'Why didn't he just ask me himself?'* He was literally standing right in front of me. My friend, on the other hand, was thrilled. She nudged me with excitement. *"Come on, it's just one date! What's the harm?"* I hesitated.

Something about it didn't sit right with me, but I couldn't quite put my finger on it. Still, she had a point. It was just one date. Nothing serious. After this weekend, I'd be flying back home, and I'd probably never see him again.

Despite my reservations, I agreed. He seems like a nice guy, I told myself. It's just one date... what could possibly happen? His name was Chris, and he had a kindness about him that instantly drew me in. He told the corniest jokes; the kind that made you roll your eyes but still smile. He was incredibly attentive, always making sure I felt seen.

His emerald-green eyes had a way of pulling me in, making me feel safe— wanted, even loved. I ignored the nagging feeling in my gut, pushing aside any doubts. *Why would I question something that felt this good?* Over the next nine months, I found myself completely immersed in the relationship.

Back in 1988, there were no cell phones, no instant messaging. We wrote letters—real, handwritten letters. The kind where you had to wait days for a response, where every envelope held a piece of someone's heart, sealed with a stamp. Every day after school, I raced to the mailbox, my heart pounding with anticipation.

The thought of receiving a letter from Chris made me feel like I was living in a real-life love story. His words were unlike anything I had ever heard before. He told me I was beautiful, smart, funny, and audacious—words that felt foreign after years of hearing the opposite from my dad. So, when Chris promised to love me for the rest of his life, I believed him. The guy I thought I'd never see again became the one I couldn't imagine life without.

He flew me up for his prom, opened doors for me, paid for dinners, and gifted me jewelry. But more than anything, he listened —really listened. And I loved to talk. Storytelling came naturally to me; my mom used to have me tell her stories to help her fall asleep. But with Chris, it was different. He didn't just listen—he hung on to every word. For the first time in my life, I felt truly loved.

He wasn't just my boyfriend. He was my safe place. He was my best friend. I poured my heart out to him, sharing every dream, every fear, every scar. He knew everything about me—every tear I had shed, every childhood trauma, every strength, and every weakness. Yet, it never occurred to me that I knew so little about him. He would share small pieces of his life, but his focus was always on me—my family, my school, my future.

He took in the wounded bird that I was, and mended my broken wing. What I didn't realize then was that I had become emotionally dependent on him. His emotions dictated mine—if he was happy, I was happy; if he was upset, I felt it too. His anger became my anger, his sadness my sorrow.

I had never experienced anything like this before. I didn't know what to call it, but it had to be love. Something powerful connected us, something I had never felt before. After a year of dating—after countless letters and an outrageous long- distance phone bill—he asked me a question that every girl dreams of hearing: *"Will you marry me?"*

My dream was finally coming true. My knight in shining armor had arrived, ready to rescue me from the dungeon I had been trapped in for so long.

I didn't know much about his family, his past, or his friends, but none of that mattered. He wanted me. He was willing to marry a girl with a painful past, to stand by my side as we took on the world together. The fairy tale was unfolding right before my eyes.

My happily ever after was finally within reach. I could hardly believe it. Chris made his intentions crystal clear—he was going to rescue me from the "hell hole" I was living in. And without hesitation, without a second thought about what lay ahead, I leaped at the chance.

I clung to him with everything I had, desperate to escape my broken home. He left everything behind for me—his family, his job, his hometown. He told me he was just one credit short of graduating high school but had dropped out because he couldn't bear to be away from me any longer.

It didn't take long for me to fall completely, head over heels, in love with him. He knew exactly what to say. When I needed love, he gave me security. When I doubted myself, he offered reassurance. When I felt broken, his shoulder was there for me to cry on. He became my everything.

Looking back now, I see all the red flags I missed. I knew almost nothing about him—there was no one in his life who could vouch for his character. He had no close friends, no strong family ties. He admitted to having been in an institution for anger issues but assured me that counseling had helped him gain control.

At the time, I believed him because he had never shown any signs of "bad" anger. Yes, he'd get upset sometimes but nothing like my dad. He rarely spoke about his past, only mentioning that he was the black sheep of his family. Yet, he was always eager to listen to everything about me. This gave him full access to every part of me—my thoughts, my fears, my dreams.

Looking back, I realize he was careful to keep his own life a mystery while saying all the right things to draw me in, making sure I fell for him completely. If I had been in a healthier emotional state, I might have recognized the warning signs.

To everyone—including myself—he appeared to be the kindest, most selfless person I had ever met. He was always willing to help, never turning anyone away. There was no hesitation, no "I can't." Every time he extended a hand to someone in need, it only reinforced how lucky I felt to have him.

He would give the shirt off his back, and to the outside world, he seemed like the perfect man.

The abuser seeks to fill a void in the person's life, offering to be a listening ear. This can also involve persuading and convincing the victim that only the abuser alone can fulfill their every need. They pretend to be someone and something they're not. They pretend to be someone you can trust, so you put your guard down. -Psychology Today

Prince Charming is the classic fairytale hero—the one who rescues the damsel in distress and embarks on a grand quest to break the evil spell. For me, the “evil” wasn’t a wicked sorcerer or a fire-breathing dragon. It was growing up in a home filled with violence, watching my mother endure beatings from an abusive, alcoholic father.

My dungeon was the daily reality of coming home to chaos, hearing over and over again that we would never amount to anything. So, when my prince charming arrived, he became my escape, my safe haven. He was the center of my world. We spent countless nights lying in the grass, gazing up at the stars, sharing our dreams for the future.

We envisioned a big house filled with laughter and children. We dreamed of traveling the country in a 5th wheel, "glamping" at every state park. We talked about retiring by the ocean, waking up to the sound of waves, and watching the sun rise and set over the water. We wanted our own happily ever after.

Nine months into our marriage, I found out I was pregnant. We were over the moon with excitement. We had always wanted to have kids young so we wouldn’t be “old” parents. Life felt like an extended honeymoon, full of hope and dreams for our growing family.

The walls I had built around myself—the ones I had carefully constructed for protection—started to come down, brick by brick. For the first time, I let myself breathe. It felt strange to lower my guard, to step out of the fortress I had hidden behind for so long, but with him, I felt safe. I trusted him with everything. He was my rock, my refuge.

Emotionally, I couldn't imagine living without him. Then, without warning, strange things began to happen. Around five months into my pregnancy, I started receiving odd phone calls at our apartment. Each time I answered, there was nothing but silence before the caller abruptly hung up.

At first, I dismissed it as a prank—maybe just a wrong number, or someone playing games. But when the calls kept coming, always at the same time each day, unease settled in. Still, I pushed the feeling aside, convincing myself it was nothing. Then on my 21st birthday—a day that was supposed to be special, my mom had come over to make me dinner, a small but meaningful celebration marking my transition into adulthood.

I remember it all so vividly. The windows were open, letting in a soft breeze. The scent of home-cooked food filled the air. I lay in bed, waiting for Chris to get home, listening to the comforting sounds of my mom and sister laughing in the kitchen. A warm sense of contentment washed over me. *This is it,* I thought. *This is what I always imagined married life would be.* But just as I allowed myself to sink into that moment, a sudden knot formed in my stomach.

My body tensed. A wave of unease crept in, the kind that made my skin crawl. I sat up, scanning the room as my breath quickened. The sensation was hauntingly familiar—the same instinctive dread I used to feel as a child when I'd come home from school and sense my father was in one of his moods.

Back then, me and Cyndee knew to disappear into our bedroom, bracing ourselves for the storm to come. And now, that same feeling had returned, uninvited and unshakable. I took a deep breath, trying to ground myself. *You're not there anymore,* I reminded myself. *This is different. You're safe.* I repeated it over and over in my mind, but no matter how many times I told myself, the unease refused to fade. Something was off—I could feel it deep in my bones.

Then, just minutes after that gut-wrenching sensation settled in, Chris walked through the door. The moment I saw him, my stomach dropped. His face was pale, almost ghostly, his expression tight with fear. My mind raced. *What's going on?*

We had been in such a good place—nothing had happened that would explain why he looked like he had just seen a ghost. Without a word, he took my hand and led me to our bedroom.

He sat me down on the bed, knelt in front of me, and gently kissed my belly. Then, he looked up, his eyes searching mine, and said, "*You know I love you, right?*"

A wave of nausea hit me. My entire body tensed. No. No, no, no I told myself. My instincts screamed that something was coming —something I wasn't prepared for. I didn't want to answer him. I didn't want to acknowledge the question because I knew, without a doubt, that whatever he was about to say next would change everything. Chris took a deep breath before finally speaking.

He explained that a few months ago, a young woman had come into the shop to get her car fixed. He had assigned her ticket to a mechanic, processed her paperwork, and thought nothing of it. But later, he found out that she had asked another employee for his number and even left hers for him. According to Chris, when he saw the message, he immediately tossed the piece of paper away. But that wasn't the end of it.

A week later, she returned. This time she specifically asked for him. He claimed he had been clear with her, telling her he was happily married and expecting a baby, but she didn't seem to care. Instead of backing off, she started showing up at his workplace regularly, making excuses to see him. Chris swore up and down that he never encouraged her.

That he never talked to her. That he wanted nothing to do with her. But as I sat there, my mind spun. If that were true, why did he look so terrified? Why was my gut telling me there was more to the story? She told him she had been trying to reach him after work, but every time I answered, she hung up.

That's when it all clicked—the mysterious calls, the uneasy feeling I couldn't shake. Chris claimed that her persistence had become too much, that she was harassing him. So, one day, he finally decided to call her and tell her to stop showing up at his job and calling our home. I wanted to ask how he got her number if he had supposedly thrown it away, but I couldn't bring myself to say the words. Right now, I just needed to hear the rest of the story. My stomach was in knots, my breathing shallow. My heart pounded so loudly in my chest; I was sure he could hear it.

I braced myself, clinging to the desperate hope that whatever he was about to say next wouldn't confirm my worst fear—that he had cheated on me. My mind was spinning, and his words became distant and numbing. I couldn't focus on what he was saying anymore. All I could hear was my father's voice, *"You will never amount to anything."* I didn't want to believe it, didn't want to let those words take root—but in that moment, they did.

Had I ended up here because I hadn't done more with my life? If I had gone to college, would I be with Chris or even in this situation now? As much as I wanted to push the thought away, I couldn't. For the first time, I felt myself breaking under the weight of the words my dad had spoken over me for years. And worst of all, at that moment, I believed them.

After a few minutes, I managed to pull myself back into the conversation. My heart pounded in my chest as I locked eyes with him. Then, in a voice barely above a whisper, he said, *"I met her at the park... and she got in my truck."* Something inside me snapped. A fire erupted from the pit of my stomach and surged upward, but instead of screaming, my voice dropped—low, steady, almost unrecognizable. *"She got in your truck... and then what?"* The silence between us grew deafening.

He hesitated, his voice barely audible. *"She kissed me... but I pushed her away. She forced herself on me."* His words twisted in my mind, but they didn't fit. *How in the hell could a 5- foot-2-inch girl force herself on you?* The detail of her height had slipped out earlier, buried somewhere in the haze of his confession.

Funny how even in the middle of blind rage, certain details refuse to be ignored. But he wasn't done. His face twisted with something between shame and fear as he muttered, *"That's not the worst part."* I remember glancing at the clock. September 20th. 4:45 PM.

A moment frozen in time. One of the biggest days of my life—shattered in an instant. Then, suddenly, we were interrupted. A sharp knock echoed through the apartment. I heard my mom answer the door; her voice sounded a little confused. A man with a badge stood there, asking for Chris.

He wasn't in uniform, making it hard to tell exactly who he was. At that very moment, the phone rang. Before I could react, Chris grabbed it. "*Hello?*" His voice was tense. A deep, angry voice on the other end cut through the silence. *"Are you Chris Moore?"* Chris hesitated. "*Uh... yeah. Who's this?"* The response was instant—and explosive *"STAY THE HELL AWAY FROM MY GIRLFRIEND OR I'LL KILL YOU!"*

The words hit me like a brick to the chest. I could hear the man's fury, even from across the room. My breath caught in my throat. My mind scrambled to make sense of it all. *Oh my God... what in the world is happening?*

I sank onto the couch as a sharp pain twisted through my stomach. The cramps grew stronger, my chest tightened, and my head spun. A nauseating wave of dizziness hit me. *This has to be a dream.* I repeated it over and over, grasping for some sense of reality. It was the only thing keeping me from completely losing control.

At the door, the man with the badge spoke in hushed tones to Chris. I couldn't make out their words, but then the man's gaze met mine. His expression was heavy—filled with something that looked like pity. My heart pounded. *What did he know that I didn't?* Chris stepped back inside, his face pale and hands shaking. His voice was uneven, barely above a whisper. *"I'm being accused of rape."* The air was sucked from the room.

My ears started ringing. Chris kept talking, his words frantic, stumbling over themselves. "This is what I was trying to tell you... before it got out of control." My entire body went cold.

"WHAT DO YOU MEAN BEFORE?" I screamed. He guided me to a chair as the blood drained from my face, leaving me just as pale as him. My body felt weightless, like I was slipping away from reality. Chris took a deep breath and continued.

He swore that when she first tried to kiss him, he pushed her away. When she tried again, he pulled back. He told her there was nothing between them, that it would never happen.

That's when, according to him, she tore her own shirt, scratched her own face, and said: *"You will pay for this."* As she opened the truck door to leave, rain started pouring down in sheets. He claimed he pulled her back inside, pleading with her not to lie, not to do this. But she just looked at him with cold certainty and said, *"One day, your wife will find out who you really are."*

Chris was finally given the chance to tell his side of the story. The detective explained that because he had allegedly threatened her—though I was never told exactly what was said—she was too afraid to appear in court. Despite multiple calls from the detective urging her to come forward, she refused, saying she just wanted to forget the whole thing had ever happened.

I remember standing outside the courtroom, wanting to go inside. I wanted to see her. I needed to know what she looked like, what kind of car she drove, where she lived. I wanted to ask her everything—but at the same time, I was terrified of the answers. When I asked the detective if I could attend, he leaned in close and spoke gently, glancing at my pregnant belly. *"Given your condition, I advise you to wait outside,"* he said.

Then, after a brief pause, he added something I would never forget: *"Rape victims rarely testify because they're afraid to face their attacker. She likely won't show, and the charges will be dropped. But in most cases, their stories are true."*

All I could focus on were the words, *"These charges will be dropped."* Everything else faded into the background, sinking into a place I knew all too well—denial. Denial was my safe haven, a locked box in my mind where I stored away anything too painful to face. If something threatened my reality, I tucked it away, sealing the lid tight as if it had never existed.

Along with it, I buried the pain, refusing to confront the truth staring me in the face. It was easier to believe the lie I told myself than to accept the reality that could shatter everything.

Chapter 4
The Mask of Denial

Denial is a defense mechanism in which an individual refuses to recognize or acknowledge objective facts or experiences. It's an unconscious process that serves to protect the person from discomfort or anxiety. - Psychology Today

For months after the *incident,* I found myself constantly searching for signs—some shred of evidence that would confirm or contradict what this woman had claimed about my husband. But nothing added up. Nothing made sense. His character remained unchanged. He was still the same thoughtful, helpful, and kind man I had always known. He made sure my car never ran out of gas, opened every door for me, dedicated songs that made me feel cherished, and introduced me to everyone as the love of his life.

Yet, the fear lingered. The police report mentioned she drove a red sedan, and from that moment on, every red sedan on the road made my stomach clench. Would I see her? Would she try to approach me? Would she come back to tear my world apart? The weight of those questions was unbearable. In the end, the only way forward was to let it go. With no proof to confirm her accusations, I forced myself to stop searching for something that wasn't there. If I wanted to move on, I had to stop seeing him as the man she claimed he was. It didn't matter what the detective said—he was wrong.

My husband was the kindest, most devoted man I had ever known. He worked tirelessly to provide for me, listened to my worries, and stood by my side through everything. He *loved* me. I refused to believe that he was anything other than the man I had built my life around. How could this woman accuse him like that? Was she delusional? A liar? A psychopath?

I clung to the parts of his story that made sense, choosing to ignore the painful possibility that I might be married to someone I didn't truly know. I shut my eyes to the doubts creeping in and made a decision—*for better or for worse, I was staying.* I convinced myself that I could make this marriage work, that love, and commitment would be enough to hold everything together. Deep down, I knew the real reason I stayed. I didn't want my children to grow up in a broken home. I wanted them to have the stability of a two-parent household—the kind of stability I never had.

And if I'm being completely honest, I was afraid. Afraid of being a single mother, of raising my children alone, of facing the unknown without him.

So, I told myself that as long as I kept my family together, I was doing the right thing—no matter the cost. As the years passed, denial became my shield against pain. It transported me back to my childhood, to the nights filled with shouting and fighting that left me frozen in fear.

Slowly, unhealthy patterns began to surface. The abuse didn't appear overnight—it crept in gradually, little by little, subtle enough to make me question whether it was even real. Because I craved love and approval, I molded myself to fit Chris's expectations. At first, it was small things—like changing how I made dinner. He wanted a three-course meal every night, no exceptions. It didn't matter if I had worked an eight-hour shift, driven across town to pick up the kids from three different schools, and barely had time to sit down. Dinner was my duty, and it had to be done. At first, I didn't mind.

I *loved* taking care of my family. But then the comments started. *"Dinner isn't hot—were you too busy to keep it warm?"* Or *"Did you run out of ideas? I swear we just ate this last week."* Each remark seemed harmless on its own, but they chipped away at me, making me question whether anything I did was ever good enough. Every remark pushed me to try harder, to prove myself, to meet his ever-changing expectations. But no matter what I did, there was always something to critique. It felt like an emotional rollercoaster—his moods dictated the atmosphere of our home. When he was happy, I felt a sense of relief; when he was down, the weight of his emotions consumed me.

I became so attuned to his feelings that, with just a single glance, I could predict how the rest of the day would unfold.

I had learned this skill long before Chris—growing up, I did the same thing with my father. I always knew whether he would ignore us or start a fight. It's amazing how we can become so accustomed to the behavior of an abuser that we learn to navigate their chaos with caution.

As Chris's mood swings intensified, so did his demands. What once seemed like minor expectations became unspoken rules I had to follow. And yet, I convinced myself it was all worth it. The fleeting moments of happiness were enough to keep me holding on, even when the bad days far outnumbered the good. His routine became predictable, driving all night, sleeping all day.

When he was home, he would shower, eat and immediately lose himself in his computer. Our conversation was few and far between. I yearned to talk to him about my day, the kids or anything at all. But his distance was deafening, leaving me constantly questioning what was really going on in his mind. He stayed online in chat rooms until the early hours of the morning.

He told me it was a great way to meet other couples to hang out with. What he didn't tell me was he was spending his time in swingers' chat rooms. He constantly watched porn, claiming it was to enhance our bedroom experiences. He would often fall asleep while the porn movies were playing. I always felt so disgusted because I didn't want my children to hear those horrible sounds the actors would make. I would wait for him to fall asleep before I went in for the night. I would tiptoe carefully, even holding my breath; just to avoid waking him. I slowly climbed into bed, one leg, then the other.

Quietly leaning back until my head softly laid on the pillow.

I pulled up the sheets all the way to my neck, hoping he'd get the hint that I wasn't interested. I trained myself to hold my breath and exhale silently. As I lay there for a few moments, I told myself "If I can just stay completely still, not move a muscle, maybe he won't notice me... and I might get through one night without any sexual contact. I let out a breath so soft, even I could barely sense it.

As my eyes began to close, I felt his hot, heavy breath against my neck. I used to love that feeling when we were dating—it would send shivers down my spine, fill my stomach with fluttering butterflies.

But now, that warmth only brought a creeping dread, settling over me like a thick, suffocating blanket. The kind that traps the air, leaving no room to breathe. What I once loved had twisted into fear. And then, the words that made my skin crawl: *"You know, whatever we do in our bedroom is okay with God because we're married. He's fine with whatever I do."*

His words unsettled me, but I hesitated to question him. Deep down, I knew what he was hinting at, and it made me feel sick. For months, he had been dropping hints about something I was completely against—an act I couldn't reconcile with love or faith. Yet, he kept insisting that it wasn't a sin—not in a marriage.

He repeated it over and over: *"God blesses what we do in our marriage bed. If it stays between us, God doesn't care."*

Countless times, I sat through his explanations of why this act would "enhance" our intimacy. I whispered a silent prayer: *"God, are You really okay with this? Isn't it a sin? Your word says so. Why does he insist it's not? And if he loves me, why do his desires make me feel so repulsed?"*

"This is a sin!" I blurted out. *"I can't do this". Trying to whisper and not wake the kids. "I can't do this".*

His response was firm: *"Do you love God?*

"Do you want to be a good wife? The Bible says you should submit to your husband. No, babe, this isn't a sin—it's only wrong between two men, not between a husband and wife. I promise, anything goes in the bedroom if it's between us."

"Or do you want me to go look for this somewhere else? I can leave right now and I know several women that will do this but I want you. I choose to do this with you."

I slid into oblivion.

I let myself disappear. I lay there, staring at the bed posts. My fists holding my bedspread, screaming on the inside. I could hear the ceiling fan spinning. It spun round and round, until everything blurred and in that moment, I was gone—detached from my own body, from my own pain.

My mind drifted far from that room, far from him.

I was at the beach, lying on warm sand, feeling the cool waves wash over my feet. The breeze carried the scent of salt, and the sky stretched endlessly above me.

The sand scratched my back, but I didn't care. I just laid there, basking in the sun, breathing in the ocean air. It was beautiful. It was peaceful. And I was numb. I didn't *feel* anything.

That night, I experienced a violation of the highest degree—I was sodomized. This was a different kind of rape. Pain I can't fully describe. Pain, I hope I can someday forget. I prayed silently, tears streaming down my face, pleading with God to understand why this was happening.

I just wanted to be a good wife. But heaven remained silent, and I felt invisible—like I didn't exist. When he finished, he told me how that could have been a better experience

but instead I had become boring. After all his hard work—providing for me, making sure I was taken care of, the only thing he asked in return was that I loved him well and made sure he was satisfied.

Crying and not understanding what had just happened, I couldn't grasp as to why it wasn't enough. Why I wasn't enough. I promised him I would do better if he just gave me another chance. Which would get him to ask the question I despised the most.

"Ok so what are you willing to do for me?" I could never tell if it was a trap, so I always responded with, "*What do you need me to do?"* Silence followed.

Then, without another word, he gently pushed me back onto the bed. *"Let's try this again,"* he murmured. A wave of nausea hit me. All I wanted was to disappear, to run and never stop, never look back.

Most nights, I cried myself to sleep, my whimpers barely more than a whisper. I carried so much pain inside, constantly wondering—was I the only one? Did other married women go through this too? And if they did, did they like it?

I knew I didn't want this, but who would understand? Who would believe me? When you repeat the same lie to yourself over and over, eventually, it becomes your truth. When you're groomed to accept love—even when it's tainted—you take it, because that's what you were taught love was supposed to be.

I grew up believing love was magical. Instead, it became my prison, and I had no idea how to escape. My voice disappeared. My opinions no longer mattered.

I did what I was told and smiled for the world to see. Everyone thought he was the perfect husband. And I was told I was the luckiest woman alive.

The abuser demands secrecy of what is going on behind closed doors. By this time, the abuser has convinced other people to believe they are charming and friendly. This usually results in the victim or victims to become fearful and unable to express their concerns to anyone. The victim feels alone, afraid and trapped. ~ Psychology Today

"What happens in this house, stays in this house." It was a phrase I heard daily for 24 years. I didn't realize it at the time, but those words were meant to keep me silent—to ensure that everything happening within our walls stayed hidden.

On the outside, we appeared to be the picture-perfect family. Chris had carefully constructed the image he wanted the world to see. We were deeply involved in our children's lives—sports, school, community events. I volunteered. Chris volunteered. Everyone knew *The Moore Family*.

To the outside world, we had it all. After years of hard work, we had finally saved enough money to build our first home. A beautiful 3,200-square-foot house—four bedrooms, two and a half baths, two living areas, a game room, and an office. It felt like a dream come true, a place where anything was possible.

On Thanksgiving morning in 2009, we stood together on the empty lot, holding hands, speaking life into the space that would soon become our home. We thanked God for this blessing, for the future we were about to build. I can still feel the overwhelming excitement of that moment—the hope, the joy, the belief that maybe, just maybe, this house would be the fresh start we needed.

As the framing went up, I carefully chose scriptures for each room, writing them across the 2x4s like prayers woven into the very foundation of our home. I walked through the skeletal structure, reading the words over and over, believing with all my heart that we were building a house of love—a place where our family could truly grow together.

This would be our forever home. The place where Chris and I would grow old side by side, where our grandchildren would one day run through the hallways, filling the rooms with laughter. We often imagined what it would be like to be grandparents, dreaming of spoiling them, creating memories, and being the "cool" grandparents that everyone adored.

In those moments, our future felt so certain, so full of promise. We laughed, we planned, and we held onto the dream that this house would be the fresh start we had always longed for.

It was the most beautiful time—one I can still picture so clearly. I remember thinking we'd need two rocking chairs for the front porch, where we'd sit and savor our first sip of coffee each morning. As I paused to take in the sky, I noticed the clouds—fluffy and white, like scattered cotton balls drifting effortlessly. A soft breeze carried the scent of fresh lumber, filling my lungs with a sense of renewal. I could finally breathe again.

Hope swelled in my heart as I listened to the kids excitedly choosing their rooms. I glanced over at Chris, watching him show them where the "game room" would be, describing all the things we'd put inside. We locked eyes, and in that moment, we knew—we had done it. After everything, we had finally made it. "We did it," we whispered to each other, and I couldn't stop the tears from spilling over. They weren't tears of sadness, but of overwhelming joy for the future we were stepping into together.

Yes, the road had been rough. There were bumps, moments of doubt, and times I questioned everything. But I held on to the hope that things could change, that *he* could change.

I've heard that when marriages begin to fall apart, there are two things' people believe might put them back together:

- First, a new baby—because somehow, a child is supposed to mend what's broken.
- Second, a new house—a fresh start, a way to leave the past behind and embrace something new.

And so, there we stood, in the middle of our brand-new beginning.

I'm not saying that babies aren't a blessing or that buying a new home is wrong. I can only share what I've learned from my own experience. I truly believed that changing our surroundings—moving somewhere new—would somehow fix our marriage.

But the truth is, no physical change can heal what's broken inside. The only one who can truly restore a marriage—or a person—is Jesus. If love has already faded, having another child in hopes of rekindling that love will only lead to heartache when nothing changes.

A new home may be a fresh start on the outside, but if the wounds remain unhealed, it's just a different place to carry the same pain. I convinced myself that building this house would bring back our happiness, that pouring our energy into something new would erase the old hurt. But it didn't.

The cracks in our foundation weren't in the walls of our home—they were in us.

After 5 months of waiting, we finally moved in. For anyone who has bought a new home, you know the feeling—one of the best in the world. The fresh scent of paint and new carpet, the countertops we carefully chose together, the brick fireplace, the beautiful new blinds—each detail making the house feel warm and inviting.

The massive pantry was more than enough for four growing teenagers. We picked the sink with Chris in mind, knowing he'd need it after working in the garage. The master bedroom was huge, and the closet was enough to fit a twin-sized bed. The front porch faced the sunrise, just as we had imagined. And yes, we bought the two rocking chairs.

That first morning, we sat there, coffee in hand, watching the sun rise over our new beginning. The sound of the kids' laughter filled the yard, echoing joy and possibility. As I stood there taking it all in, I knew—I was living one of the happiest moments of my life. Then, everything changed. I became invisible again.

My voice—what was left of it—was silenced. It didn't happen overnight. It didn't even happen in a few years. It was a slow, calculated process—years of love bombing, of being made to feel like I was the only woman in the world for him.

He made me believe I was special, irreplaceable. Over and over, I heard the same words: *He could never live without me.*

I didn't understand it then, but those words became ingrained in my mind. I truly believed he would never let me go—no matter what. For a short time, the sexual abuse stopped. I finally found solace when I was in my bedroom, I would gaze out through the two large bay windows at the breathtaking view.

For a little while, I had peace. Those fleeting moments of calm were etched into my memory, and I clung to them. Then came the day everything changed. People often say someone *flipped a switch* —a sudden shift, a turning point. I didn't recognize it at the time, but that was the day he changed forever.

It was the Fourth of July. My oldest son's girlfriend had invited us over for dinner before heading to the countryside to set off fireworks. The evening started well enough, but something felt off. There was a heaviness in the air, an unshakable sense of unease. I couldn't explain it, but deep down, I knew— something was about to happen.

My son and his girlfriend had a small disagreement—something trivial, the kind of thing teenagers argue about. To this day, I can't even remember what it was. As we got ready to leave for the fireworks, Chris told everyone to get in the car. We climbed in, and almost immediately, he started drilling Justin, my oldest, about what had happened.

Justin didn't want to talk—typical for a teenager—but Chris wouldn't let it go. I was driving. Justin and Josh sat behind us, with Jeremy and Jess in the third row. The more Chris pushed, the heavier his voice became. I felt it instantly—the tension in the air, the way my body reacted before my mind even caught up.

My hands started to shake. My breathing slowed down while the knots in my stomach tightened. My heart pounded, the sound of it growing louder in my ears. I gripped the steering wheel tighter and tighter, watching as my knuckles turned white.

I tried to focus on the road, but dizziness crept in. Then, out of nowhere, Chris erupted.

"TELL ME WHAT HAPPENED!"

This wasn't just raised voices. It was rage—pure, unfiltered, like something had taken over him. It felt like a volcano on the verge of eruption. I glanced at Josh, who locked eyes with me. He didn't say a word, but his look almost seemed to whisper, *Mom, it's going to be okay.* I took a deep breath, trying to steady myself.

Then, in an instant, Chris started yanking at his seatbelt, thrashing, trying to turn around and grab Justin. His arms moving violently, as if he was swinging at someone who wasn't even there. His entire body jerked with such force that I struggled to keep control of the car. *"STOP!"* I shouted, my voice cracking. Jess sobbed. *"Stop, Dad! Please, stop!"*

Jeremy sat frozen, tears streaming down his face. He couldn't even form words. Justin, just 17 years old, fought to hold Chris back, trying to keep him restrained as he thrashed and pushed, desperately to break free.

It was chaos. Josh sat still—silent, detached. His eyes turned glassy, distant, like he had checked out of reality. He never screamed, never cried, never moved. I finally managed to pull over to the side of the road. My hands shook as I turned, scanning the backseat, desperate to make sure the kids were okay. But Chris wasn't stopping. His entire body convulsed with rage.

His head slammed against the dashboard as he jerked back and forth, like he had lost all control. It almost looked like a seizure, except it wasn't. To this day, I don't know how he never got out of that seatbelt. It should have unbuckled. It should have snapped free. But somehow, it didn't. Justin, Jeremy, and Jess were all crying.

Josh and I just sat there, expressionless. It was as if we had disconnected completely, burying every emotion deep within, locking them away where they couldn't reach us. We didn't cry. we didn't yell.

We couldn't even process what had just happened. Minutes later, Justin's girlfriend's family pulled over several feet ahead of us. Her dad stepped out of the car and started walking toward us, concern written all over his face. But before he could get too close,

Chris snapped back to reality, his voice eerily calm as he told me to let them know we wouldn't be coming—that something had come up. I slowly got out of the car, meeting them halfway. I kept apologizing, my words stumbling out as I told them we wouldn't be able to make it.

Then, as if the last few minutes had never happened—as if he hadn't just been violently shaking, screaming, and thrashing in his seat—Chris rolled down the window, flashed a smile, and casually waved. "*Maybe next time,*" he said. I turned to look at him. *Who was this person?*

How could he just turn it off like that? Just minutes ago, he was trying to choke our son, completely out of control. And now? Now he was calm, composed—smiling, even. As if nothing had happened. It wasn't his outburst that terrified me the most. It was how effortlessly he could shut it off, as though it had never happened at all.

The ride home was quiet, and the silence felt deafening. From the back seat, I could still hear the soft whimpers of Jess and Jeremy. Justin kept apologizing—over and over—blaming himself, promising it would never happen again. Josh said nothing. I said nothing. Chris sat facing forward, never acknowledging a word Justin said.

It was as if he hadn't just shattered the entire night. Those twenty minutes felt like an eternity. I whispered silent prayers, barely moving my lips. *God, please help us. I don't know what's coming next.*

As we pulled into the driveway, everyone moved slowly, hesitant —like stepping into the unknown. Chris sat outside for nearly an hour before finally making his way through the garage to find me. His face was unreadable, but his words cut straight through me. *"This is all Justin's fault,"* he said. *"If he had just listened to me from the start, I never would have reacted that way."* I stared at him, stunned. *Was he really saying this?*

My voice came out sharper than I intended. *"Justin is a teenager. YOU are an adult."* He ignored me. Instead, he called for Justin to come downstairs. When Justin appeared, Chris's tone remained cold and controlled. *"Next time I ask you to talk, you'd better do it fast."* Justin stood there, his face pale, his expression sullen.

He looked stunned, like he was still trying to process everything that just happened. *"Yes, sir,"* he finally murmured, then hesitantly he stepped forward, trying to hug Chris—searching for reassurance, for some sign that things were okay. Chris would not hug him back. The rejection settled over the room like a heavy weight, thick and suffocating. Justin felt it. I felt it. Then came the final blow.

"We don't need to be telling people what happened today. We don't go around sharing our business. It would be embarrassing if anyone found out how Justin acted." His voice was firm unwavering. "What Happens in this house stays in this house."

The next morning, Chris woke up, and the entire house was on edge. We moved carefully, being cautious of every word, every step—unsure of what to expect. No one knew how to act or what to say.

Breakfast was eerily silent. You could hear the clinking of silverware, the occasional rustle of movement, but not a single word was spoken. The air felt thick. Then, out of nowhere, Chris broke the silence. *"Why is everyone so quiet? You're acting like someone died or something."*

He had no idea how true those words were. Someone *had* died. The Chris we once knew—the one we thought we knew—was gone.

In his place stood someone else entirely, someone unrecognizable. And that moment marked the beginning of our world turning upside down. From the outside, we were still the *perfect* family.

A beautiful home, a brand- new Suburban, a manicured lawn—we looked like we had it all. And we smiled, even when we were breaking inside. But behind closed doors, the cracks were becoming harder to hide. The abuse grew more rigid, more visible.

Every day felt like walking a tightrope, never knowing which version of Chris we would get. Would it be the caring, loving, and kind Chris? Or the one who could turn in an instant, without warning? Abuse isn't simple—it doesn't follow a single pattern.

Chris had a different way of breaking each of us. With Josh, it was control masked as discipline. His task was cleaning the downstairs bathroom, and if Chris found even the tiniest speck of dirt—no matter how spotless it already was—Josh had to start over. Baseboards, floors, everything. Sometimes he had to clean it three times before he was allowed to stop.

Almost every time, he had done it right from the start. But Chris wasn't looking for a job well done; he was looking for failure. Instead of seeing the big picture, he searched for flaws, for reasons to make Josh feel like his efforts were never enough.

I believe that stayed with Josh—the relentless need for approval buried deep inside, pushing him toward an invisible, unreachable goal. *"If I can just reach the next level, maybe then I'll be good enough"*. But the truth was, no matter how high he climbed, the approval never came from his dad.

For Justin, it was different, yet just as cruel. Chris dangled validation in front of him like crumbs on a trail. Because Justin was good with his hands, Chris loved teaching him things—how to change a tire, how to paint, how to work with wood.

I watched the pride in Justin's face when he completed a task for his dad, searching for that moment of recognition. But it never lasted. Chris always followed up with, *"Well, if I had done it, I would've done it this way,"* or *"You could've done better if..."*

The approval came in small doses. just enough to give Justin hope —only to be torn away again. No matter how hard he tried, no matter how much effort he put in, criticism always followed.

I believe that left a deep void in Justin, one that made him crave validation, made him fight to be seen. Because no matter what he did, it was never enough.

Jeremy, the youngest of the three boys, didn't experience his father's abuse until he became a teenager. A quiet and introspective child, he kept to himself and never caused trouble. He was incredibly disciplined—completing his homework without being asked, sticking to a set bedtime, and never missing a Cross-Country practice. School was a priority for him, and his strong work ethic reflected in his excellent grades. He was the kind of son any parent would be proud of. But in Chris's eyes, Jeremy's quiet nature made him a target. Because Jeremy was quiet and not overly interested in dating, Chris perceived him as weak.

Despite the fact that Jeremy had shown interest in a few girls, it didn't align with Chris's definition of being a man. One night, Chris sat me down and insisted that no son of his was going to be "gay". I pushed back, explaining that Jeremy was simply focused on his future—his sports, his academics—and that he would find the right person when the time was right.

He was a homebody, happiest spending time with me and Jess, watching movies when he wasn't training or studying. But Chris refused to accept that. A few days later, he took it upon himself to "teach" Jeremy how to be a man.

He introduced him to pornography, claiming it would prepare him for relationships and show him what it meant to be a man. What Chris didn't realize—or didn't care about—was the lasting damage it would cause. Jeremy, who had always planned to save himself for marriage, became addicted, to porn.

He carried that guilt and struggled in silence for years. It wasn't until he fully surrendered his life to the Lord that he was able to break free. I had no idea what Chris had done, nor the weight Jeremy had been carrying. All I knew was that Chris had claimed to "set him straight" after a long talk. I assumed it was just the usual birds-and-bees discussion. I couldn't have been more wrong.

Jess's abuse didn't begin until years later, but what I didn't realize was that Chris had been secretly grooming her since she was just six years old. It started with small requests—asking her to come into the room and rub his feet, claiming it helped him relax and fall asleep.

At the time, it seemed innocent. But as the years passed, those requests slowly escalated into something far more disturbing—a reality I will uncover in the chapters to come.

For me, the abuse never truly stopped. While the vile acts became less frequent, he always found new ways to control me. The mental, psychological, and verbal torment was relentless, though often disguised in subtlety, making me question my own sanity. No matter what I did, it was never enough. I wasn't good enough in bed, never meeting his expectations.

My cooking lacked creativity—serving the same meals each week was unacceptable, and I was constantly pressured to make something more exciting.

If I spoke to the boys' coaches about their grades or progress in practice, I was accused of having ulterior motives, of seeking out an affair. It didn't matter that I maintained firm boundaries; he made me feel as if I were always on the verge of betraying him. And yet, I was the jealous one. Any time he spoke to another woman—sometimes even the mothers of our son's teammates—I was painted as possessive and insecure.

The accusations never stopped. Then, there were the moments that kept me hanging on.

Some days, he would bring home flowers, showering me with compliments, telling me he was the luckiest man alive and that he couldn't imagine where he'd be without me. Those were the breadcrumbs I survived on—small, fleeting glimpses of affection that barely sustained me. I was starving. Starving for love. Starving for something real. I convinced myself that the brief moments of happiness were worth a lifetime of suffering.

There was one instance when I discovered that a single mom from the football team had approached him, seeking an affair. He denied it, of course, but every time I volunteered at the concession stand during games, she was always there—hovering close to him, always within arm's reach.

It wasn't just her. No matter where we went, there always seemed to be a woman he knew. And he always had a perfectly reasonable explanation for why he was talking to them—helping someone through a divorce, supporting a grieving mother, boosting someone's confidence.

Each excuse sounded noble, and I wanted to believe him. I convinced myself he had boundaries. I told myself he would never cheat. I clung to the lie I needed to survive. But it kept happening. Everywhere we went, he would inevitably run into a woman he knew. The strangest part... He almost never introduced me.

His excuse was always the same—he had forgotten their name and didn't want to make them feel uncomfortable. *Them* feel awkward? What about me? What about how *I* felt? And then came the speech he gave me when he had to prove he was right. I heard it more times than I could count.

"If I truly wanted to have an affair, I could. But I don't... ""I come home to you". You should be grateful, he said, *"because instead of spending my nights at the bars, I choose every single night, to come home to my family." "But again, your insecurity and jealousy cause me to not want to be around you so if you want ALL of me, then stop making a mountain out of a molehill."*

It never failed. After his speech, I was made to feel like I was the control freak. Like I was the one who was crazy and ungrateful. So, I would cry and beg for forgiveness. His lies became my reality, and his version of the truth made his lies sound ridiculous.

Was I the one losing my grip? Was I overreacting? Had I really become the jealous, controlling wife who didn't trust her *loving* and *caring* husband?

His porn addiction had spiraled. Night after night, I would find him glued to the computer until the early hours of the morning. Sometimes, I would sneak downstairs just to see what he was doing because he wasn't coming to bed when he was home. Was he pulling away from me? Was he trying to create more distance between us?

For so long, I had begged him to stop hurting me. And yet, the strangest thing was—I missed him. I missed his presence next to me. As much as he made me feel dirty and inadequate, I couldn't imagine my life without him. I needed him. I depended on him financially. And, more than anything, I was terrified of being alone. Even if being alone meant freedom.

Even if it meant escaping the life of living with a Porn addict.

Chapter 6
Manipulation Under the Disguise of Love

At this stage, groomers will use whatever tools they have to keep their victim dependent on the groomer's power. Some methods for this might be gaslighting or destroying self-esteem. They may use guilt or other emotional manipulation to make themselves appear innocent. One example of this would be that whenever you are hurt by something they've done, and you try to communicate with them about it, it somehow ends up with you feeling bad and possibly apologizing for how unfair you've been to the groomer, who is just trying to take care of you. ~for trauma survivors.com

I had poured everything I had into him. All I wanted was for Chris to get better—to seek help, to change. Every day, my prayers were the same: "*Lord, please heal Chris from his porn addiction. Please speak to him about getting counseling. Please help him become the father and husband You created him to be.*" I convinced myself that if I prayed hard enough, if I fasted, if I worshipped, if I filled our home with scripture—if I just *loved him more*—maybe it would be enough.

What else could I do? How could I be a better wife? How could I make him see that *I* was enough? Why couldn't he recognize that he had a good woman standing right in front of him?

I had done everything I knew to do. I was loyal. I was faithful. I never cheated. I *chose* to love him, through better and worse. I stayed when he became addicted to cocaine. I stayed when he spent his nights in topless bars. I stayed even when I suspected there were other women, though I never had proof. I cooked. I cleaned. I supported him. I spoke life into him. I was his biggest cheerleader. I served him hand and foot. I even uprooted my entire life—left my family, my church, my community—just so we could stay together.

I remember the first time he raped me. But I didn't recognize it as rape— because that doesn't happen to married women, right? I had seen so many movies showing what rape was supposed to look like. A stranger lurking in the shadows, a violent attack, a helpless woman with no way to fight back. I would watch, urging the victim to run, to get help, to go to the police.

And when she didn't, I never understood why. *Why is she afraid?* I would think. *If that were me, I'd go straight to the cops the first chance I got.* But then it happened to me. And I didn't run. I didn't even realize I *should*. .

According to Webster's Dictionary, rape is defined as:

A crime, typically committed by a man, of forcing another person to have sexual intercourse against their will. I had said *no* —over and over. It *was* against my will. Every sexual act he forced on me was born from his sick fantasies—not mine. But no matter how many times I replayed it in my mind, I couldn't make sense of all this. I was slowly disappearing, fading into myself. The only way to survive was to focus on something—anything—outside of what was happening to me.

So, I counted the ceiling fan blades as they spun. One, two, three, four... or was it five? I started over, again and again, until everything else in the room blurred into nothing except that fan. Every so often, my eyes would drift to the glowing numbers on the digital clock beside me. *Maybe it'll only be 15 minutes this time.* I whispered to myself: *Just focus, Chrissie. Keep counting. Keep breathing. Just keep breathing.*

I am fully awake, yet I felt my body going numb from the waist down. I was slipping away little by little. If I was lucky, he would fall asleep right after, which gave me a chance to go cry in the shower. That was my go-to place. Where no one could hear me but God. Sometimes telling him NO, only caused it to be rougher and longer. I chose to surrender quietly to lessen the pain. Chris had a free pass to sexually abuse me any way he chose to because NO was not an option. So many thoughts would go swirling around in my head while I was getting raped. It helped me to disconnect from what was really going on.

It wasn't until years later that I learned about marital rape and the different kinds there were. What I experienced was:

- Force-only rape – this type of rape happens when physical violence is NOT present. As with all rape, this type of spousal rape is spurred by a desire to exert power and control over another person. This desire manifests in acting as if sex is an entitlement.~Healthyplace.com

I had no idea that saying NO to the violent acts he forced me to do was considered marital rape.

Sexual assault is not always overtly violent. This means that the use of force isn't the only thing that makes this assault a violation of someone's integrity~ Psych Central

The morning after was the hardest. He always wanted to talk about what happened the night before, asking if he was good, , pressing me to describe which part I liked the most. I knew he did it on purpose. He wanted the details, wanted me to say the words out loud.

I always found an excuse to avoid the conversation—usually pointing out that the kids were around. But whenever we were alone, he wouldn't let it go. Over and over, he would ask how his performance was. My silence wasn't an answer, so I had to pretend I liked it and tell him how wonderful he was. No matter how many times we had sex, he was never satisfied. He always needed more.

The sexual acts would make me sick to my stomach, but he never seemed to care or get the hint. After dropping the kids off at school, I would sit in my car trying to process the night before. I'd sit in the parking lot before work, taking a few moments to reset—and put my mask back on. I had mastered the art of pretending. I knew how to smile, how to make everything *look* okay. And for the rest of the day, no one would know the difference. I liked going to work. It demanded my full attention, leaving no space for my mind to wander into the darkness of my reality.

Every day, I followed a strict schedule—I had to plan everything precisely. Timing was everything. Leave work at exactly 4:00 PM. Pick up Jeremy from middle school practice. Head straight to the high school to get Justin and Josh. Jess took the bus, so she was home alone until I arrived. Raced home. Make tea—Chris needed it for work. Start dinner while going over the kids' schedules for the week.

PTA meeting. Booster club meeting. Football games. Softball practice. All of it swirling through my mind as I stirred pots and prepped plates.

I glanced at the clock. 5:50 PM. I picked up the pace. The tea wasn't cold enough, so I set it in the freezer for a few minutes. Dinner simmered on the stove—was it a full three-course meal? It *had* to be. Chris wouldn't settle for anything less. Meat, vegetables, starch. Maybe a roll.

Another glance at the clock. 6:04 PM. A familiar knot tightened in my stomach. "Go change," I told the kids, my voice a little too sharp. I turned the stove off, rushing to finish before—The alarm chimed. 6:05 PM.

A wave of nausea hit me. I wasn't done. I wasn't *ready* I thought I had timed everything perfectly, down to the second. But here I was—still not done. I rushed into the room to make sure there was a clean towel in the bathroom. Chris was already in the shower. He heard me come in. *"Did you put a clean towel for me?" "Yes, I did, babe. It's on the counter." "Is dinner ready?" "Yes, it's ready."*
"Is it served?" "No I was waiting for you to get out of the shower so it doesn't get cold." The water stopped. *"Well, I'm done. Go get the kids."*

I bolted out of the bathroom, called the kids downstairs, and hurried to serve everyone as fast as possible. Then we sat in silence at the table—waiting for him to come out of the bedroom. He sat down, and we all began to eat. The boys, starving from football practice, ate in silence—no one spoke until Chris did. Then, he looked up at me. *"Hey, did you say you turned the food off before I got in the shower or after?"* I froze. My mind scrambled to remember what I had just told him. My thoughts tangled; my words stuck in my throat. "*Um... I'm pretty sure I turned it off right before I walked into the room,*" I answered carefully.

"*Then why is it cold?*" My heartbeat quickened. "*It's cold? "I swear I covered it up to keep it hot. Let me warm it up in the microwave really quick...*" The boys glanced at me; *"Mine is fine, Mom,"* Jeremy said. Chris mumbled under his breath- *"Well, at least yours is warm, but mine is cold."* He slowly pushed his chair back from the table, letting out an irritated scoff before stomping off to the bedroom and slamming the door behind him.

It's chilling how an abuser can twist the narrative, painting themselves as the victim while making you doubt your own reality.

I walked in cautiously, uncertain of how he would react. He was getting dressed, his movements rigid with frustration. I didn't say a word. The air in the room grew colder with each passing second. As he bent down to tie his laces, I lowered myself to the floor beside him. This was my unspoken way of taking the blame, even when I didn't understand what I had done wrong. Most of the time, I never did. He acted as if I didn't exist, his silence louder than any outburst. And in that moment, kneeling beside him, it hit me—this was me *begging* to be seen.

At first, he ignored me. Then, without lifting his head, he finally looked up. "*I ask for one simple thing, and you can't even do that. How hard is it? Do I need to do it myself to show you how it's done?*" In my mind, I could see myself yelling at him "YES! DO IT YOURSELF. Tell me if you can go from downtown Fort Worth to two different schools, rush home, start cooking, and have it all done before you wake up. "YES, YOU DO IT. YOU FREAKING DO IT."

But none of those words left my lips. They stayed trapped inside me, caged by fear. I didn't dare let them slip out. Still staring at the floor, desperate for him to acknowledge me, I apologized—over and over again. After what felt like an eternity, he finished tying his laces and walked out of our bedroom.

I stayed on the floor, tears falling as I retraced every step in my mind, searching for where my "timing" had failed—determined to find a way to avoid making the same mistake again. "Should I have left at 3:45 instead of 4:00? Maybe I need to rethink the menu for the week? Should I keep the food on low next time so it stays hotter? Can I get home a little earlier tomorrow? Maybe the boys can catch a ride?"

My thoughts—my relentless cycle of self-blame—were suddenly interrupted by the sound of him calling for me. I quickly wiped away my tears, composing myself as best as I could before going to see what he wanted. *"Where is my tea?"* Chris asked.

Oh God I thought, I had left it in the freezer to cool and forgot to take it out. I rushed to the kitchen, pulling it out as quickly as I could. I poured it into his blue and white Coleman jug, adding plenty of ice. My hands were shaking slightly as I worked. Just as I finished, his voice cut through the air again. *"Did you make my coffee?"* A sharp cramp twisted in my stomach.

My mind scrambled, but I couldn't remember. Had I made it? Had I forgotten? My thoughts were so jumbled, so scattered, I could barely think straight. I turned to look at Jess, my heart was pounding. She took it upon herself to tell him *"Dad, Mom did make your coffee," she said. "It's already in your thermos—the green one. It's behind you."*

I think she could see the look on my face. A wave of relief washed over me, so strong I swore the entire room could feel it. I fought to keep my emotions in check, but my lips trembled, and before I could stop them, tears slipped down my cheeks. I turned quickly, grabbing a towel by the sink, wiping them away before anyone could see. But it was too late. All the kids could see me. They looked just like I did, wanting to tell him something but no one dared.

Chris said goodbye to everyone, reminding me that he'd call once he got to work. It was our routine—to always check in and let each other know we'd arrived safely. I forced a smile, hugged him, and held myself together as best I could. As the door closed behind him, the kids turned to look at me.

They knew. They had always known—the pain I tried so hard to hide, the silent suffering I never spoke of. Without saying a word, they reassured me in the only way they knew how. With their quiet gestures and understanding eyes, they let me know—my cooking was never the problem- *"Mom, we loved dinner,"* they reassured me. *"And it wasn't even cold."* One by one, they took their paper plates, tossed them in the trash, and headed upstairs to play video games.

Jess stayed behind. She sat with me, watching me closely, then in a soft voice she whispered, *"You're a good mom,"* Somehow, the kids could see it—the misery I tried so hard to hide. They felt my pain, my disappointment. They noticed how the vibrance in my eyes had faded, how the light in me had dimmed. It was the same look I had seen in my mother's eyes when I was a child, the same look she wore as my dad spoke to her the way Chris spoke to me. As a little girl, I had always admired my mom, believing she was capable of anything.

But watching the way my dad treated her; I saw that admiration wasn't enough to keep her light from fading. And now, I understood. I knew what it felt like to be her, to see myself the way she must have seen herself. No matter how many times we told her she was doing a great job, our words could never drown out the ones my dad used to tear her down. That same look of disappointment—the one I had seen in her eyes—was now staring back at me in the mirror. Chris called to say he had arrived safely and was getting ready to leave the hub. I started getting ready for bed. Maybe he was okay now. Maybe, for once, I wouldn't have to sit through a two-hour lecture.

As I lay down, I glanced at the clock—9 p.m. I let out a deep sigh, trying to process everything that had happened just hours earlier. Slowly, the heaviness in my chest began to lift. My body, always tense, finally started to relax. My eyes grew heavier, and for the first time that day, I felt like I could breathe again. I closed my eyes.

It felt like only seconds had passed when my phone started ringing. Half-asleep, I didn't answer. Then it rang again. This time, I felt my body waking up. With one eye opened, I reached for my cell phone. Seven missed calls. Not one. Seven. I cringed. The weight came crashing back—the familiar pressure, like an elephant sitting on my chest. I struggled to breathe. I called him back. Straight to voicemail.

I called again. Voicemail. I knew this game. He thought I had ignored him, and now he was punishing me for it. On the third call, he finally answered. *"I could've been dead in a ditch, and you wouldn't have known,"* he snapped. *"Because you don't know how to answer the damn phone."* He kept me awake until 3 a.m.—lecture time. Over and over, he repeated the same lines: He could leave me for someone else, but he *chose* me. He could be out at the bars, getting drunk and picking up women, but he *chose* me. Women hit on him all the time, and he could have anyone he wanted, but he ignored them—because he *chose* me. Same speech, different night. I only half-listened.

The rest of his words blurred together as I nodded along, pretending to agree, too exhausted to argue. I lost count of how many times I apologized. Each "I'm sorry" only fed his anger, dragging the conversation deeper into the night. I just wanted it to end. Finally, I begged him to let me sleep, promising to do better.
And like clockwork, he ended the call with his final demand: *What will you do for me so that I feel better?"*

Even after the grooming process is complete, the groomer will often continue to exploit and manipulate the victim. They may use their power and control to engage in further abusive behaviors, such as sexual exploitation or financial manipulation. The groomer's goal is to maintain their dominance over the victim and to fulfill their own selfish desires, regardless of the harm inflicted on the victim.~playeditwell.com

It's hard to believe that the person you once loved has become a stranger. I felt trapped—not by love, but by the twisted version of what he claimed to give me. I was bound to him, dependent on him for everything, constantly chasing his approval. He told me he loved me, then he would abuse me mentally, verbally and sexually. How was I supposed to understand what love really was? What a healthy relationship was supposed to look like? I asked myself over and over: *If I leave, where would I go? How would I survive? Who would believe me?*

I convinced myself that staying was the *right* thing to do—the Christian thing. Divorce was a sin, wasn't it? Leaving would tear the family apart. The kids would grow up without a father, and I would be alone. But if staying was the right thing to do...

Why did it hurt so much?

I would secretly draft mock budgets, trying to see if I could make it on my own. But no matter how I crunched the numbers, it was never enough. I felt trapped—not just financially, but emotionally and mentally. I had no one to turn to. The only people I was truly close to were my mom and my sister, Cyndee. But they had no idea what was happening behind closed doors.

Because "*What happens in this house, stays in this house*"

All I wanted was peace. To live without fear, without constantly looking over my shoulder. I wanted to not live on a timeline. I was exhausted from pretending to love him. Even at football games, when he wrapped his arm around me, it felt staged—just for show. To everyone else, he was the devoted husband, the lucky man who always bragged about me with a smile on his face.

But as soon as we got home, the mask came off. And the battle would begin. I remember one night, I worked late and left the dishes in the sink, telling myself I'll do them in the morning. I was exhausted. And I was safe because Chris wouldn't be home until late the next day. I thought I had time. I was wrong.

The one time I left dishes in the sink he came home early. I remember being in a heavy sleep from the long day. I felt a light nudge on my shoulder. "*Babe, wake up, I'm home, babe wake up*". I slowly opened my eyes and was shocked to see him next to me in bed. He said, *"Get up, I want to show you something. "Now?* I asked. *"Can't it wait, I'm so tired". No, babe, it can't wait. It'll only take a few seconds, I promise."*

I sat up slowly, a flicker of excitement stirred in my chest. *"Maybe he had a surprise for me? Maybe he bought me flowers?"* Rubbing my tired eyes, I followed him downstairs. But as I stepped into the kitchen, I saw nothing—no flowers, no surprise. Just him, standing by the sink.

He put his arms around my shoulders and pointed. *"What's wrong with this picture?"*

I followed his gaze. Two dirty dishes sat in the sink. My heart dropped. My stomach twisted. I swallowed hard, convinced he could hear me. *"I got off work late and figured I'd do them in the morning before you got home,"* I said, carefully". He stared at me. *"Well, I'm home."* Silence stretched between us.

"Do you want me to do it now?" I asked hesitantly. *"No,"* he said. *"I want you to stand here and think about it for a while."* He said with his sarcastic voice.

I washed the dishes, dried them, and put them away. *"See? That wasn't so hard, was it?" "No, it wasn't."* He continued, his voice calm, almost condescending. *"If you had just taken a few seconds to do it when you finished eating, we wouldn't be here right now, right?" "You're right. I'm sorry."* Without another word, he let me go back to bed.

I lay there, staring at the ceiling, replaying the moment over and over. How could I have been so naive to think he was bringing me a surprise? I waited for him to come upstairs.

Eventually, he did—going through the same routine as always. When he was finished, he rolled over, drifted off to sleep, and that was the last night he ever raped me. I couldn't quite put my finger on it, but something had changed. Something was different.

I remember wondering, *is he having an affair? Does he have someone else?* And though I felt relieved that he no longer forced himself on me, the mental, emotional, and psychological abuse never stopped. Just when I thought I had a grasp on reality, he would blindside me—twisting situations until I questioned my own sanity. *Am I crazy?* I asked myself over and over. *Am I imagining this?*

I tried to convince myself I wasn't crazy. But when he started coming home late or leaving right after dinner—only to return long after everyone was asleep—I couldn't help but wonder what he was doing. Oddly enough, even though the thought of being with him made me sick to my stomach, I still found myself questioning whether I was *enough* for him. *Maybe I should've just let him do whatever he wants with me,* I thought. *Maybe then he wouldn't need to find it somewhere else?*

Whenever I questioned his late-night trips to the store or the extra nights spent in Oklahoma motels, he'd brush me off—accusing me of being jealous and insecure. I would replay his stories in my head, over and over, trying to make sense of them. But they never quite added up. Still, he was so convincing that I started to doubt myself instead.

Even with the evidence right in front of me, I couldn't see it. I had lived in denial for so long that the line between truth and lies was completely blurred.

I prayed constantly, but this time, my prayer changed.

"Lord, open my eyes to the real truth. Give me the strength to face it, no matter how painful it may be. I'm afraid of what I might discover, but I can't keep living in a lie."

Every Friday night was family night—movies and popcorn were our tradition. The older boys would invite their friends or girlfriends, while Jeremy set up downstairs. I was in the kitchen getting snacks ready, and Jess, at ten years old, was by my side as always, eager to help.

As I pulled the popcorn from the microwave, I glanced down at her. She stared up at me with those big, beautiful brown eyes. *"Are you okay?"* I asked.

She hesitated for a moment before quietly saying she needed to tell me something. Without thinking, I gently assured her we could talk later since the movie was about to begin.

From the living room, Chris called out, asking if Jess was going to sit with him or me. She answered quickly—too quickly.

"I'm sitting with Mom tonight." I looked over and winked at her. *"You can sit with Dad if you want. I won't be upset."*

She lowered her gaze to the floor, then back up at me as if to say, *"Help me mommy"*. I wish I had seen it then. I wish I could say my intuition kicked in. I wish I had seen the hurt in her eyes. But I didn't. I smiled at her, gave her a hug and said, *"Its ok Jess, you can sit with me next week. I promise I won't be mad. Besides, we both know who your favorite is"*.

She hesitated before softly saying, *"Okay,"* and we all made our way to the living room. I settled onto the couch with Jeremy, while the boys took the opposite couch. It was a chilly night, so we brought down all the blankets. Chris, sat in his favorite rocker, looked at Jess and asked her to come sit with him.

A few days passed, and just as I was about to step into the shower, my phone rang. It was Chris. His voice was tense as he told me he'd been in an accident. He had been a truck driver for years without any incidents, but this time, there was no leniency —they let him go. Just like that, he was unemployed.

We talked it over and decided he would take a six-month break. After years on the road, he felt a pause would be beneficial. To keep us afloat, I took on two part-time jobs in addition to my full-time position at the school district. It was an incredibly difficult time. The more I worked, the less I was home.

Eventually, I even cashed in the only retirement savings I had, just to keep us going. The only time I saw the kids, was during a game or at night when I came home. Because I was working 2 jobs, by the time my shifts were over, all I wanted to do was sleep.

I couldn't believe I was trying to hold us afloat. The 6-month mark had passed, and Chris refused to find a job. We argued every day. He constantly accused me of not giving him a moment to breathe, insisting that he was overworked and exhausted.

He never missed a chance to remind me how stressed he was, telling me it was my turn to hold down the fort. The arguments escalated when I finally reached my breaking point. I told him I couldn't keep working three jobs. Either he found work, or I was leaving. For the first time, I heard myself say it.

I couldn't believe it. I had finally found a sliver of courage to say the words I had been too afraid to say before; "I will leave". Then, just when I thought I had taken control of the situation, the rug was pulled out from under me.

One weekday night, as I was getting ready for bed, I was about to step into the shower when I realized I hadn't seen Jess in a while. The TV was off, and the house was extra quiet. I knew Jeremy was still at a Cross-Country meet, but something felt... off.

I climbed the stairs, each step making my chest tighten against the unsettling silence. The house felt eerily still, almost unnatural. As I reached the top, I scanned the game room—no sounds, no movement. Something was wrong.

As I walked past the couch, it felt like a fist slammed into my stomach, knocking the air from my lungs. I was caught somewhere between shock and disbelief.

There they were. It felt like I had stepped into a scene from a movie—one I desperately wished wasn't real. Jess was on the couch laying on her back, and Chris—he was on his knees, leaning towards her private area. His head was tilted downward, and for a split second, I assumed he was checking on Jess—maybe she had a stomachache. From where I stood, it looked like he was leaning over her belly. He hadn't noticed I was standing there. But the moment he did, he jolted, whipping his head around like a deer caught in headlights.

"She said her tummy was hurting," he blurted out. *"I was just checking to see if it was serious."* His face was slick with sweat, his eyes distant—almost vacant—like he was trapped in some sort of trance. His hands fidgeted, restless, as if he couldn't figure out where to put them.

I swallowed hard, my throat tightening as I turned to Jess. She sat up slowly, her face empty—like she had retreated somewhere far away. I knew that look. I knew it too well. It was the same look I had worn for years.

A wave of nausea rolled over me. *"Do you want to come with me to the bathroom?"* I asked her softly. Relieved- she stood up and followed me.

Chris looked at me and scoffed, *"Well since you're finally here to check on her, I'll be downstairs in the garage smoking a cigarette."* I stayed still, waiting to hear the door shut behind him. Once I was sure he was gone, I closed the bathroom door and sat down on the cold, clammy tile floor. My mind spiraled, racing through the worst possible scenarios.

Jess looked at me, her voice quiet but firm. *"Mom, I need to tell you something."* Every muscle in my body tensed. I swallowed hard, praying I could hold myself together for whatever she was about to say.

Somehow, deep down, I already knew. But I still clung to the hope that I was wrong. Jess looked straight into my eyes—not with fear, not with sadness, but with relief.

Those beautiful brown eyes. The same ones that met mine the moment she was born. I remembered it so clearly—the doctor placing her on my chest, her tiny head lifting just enough for our eyes to lock. In that instant, nothing else existed. No words were spoken, but I felt her heartbeat, steady and strong. Her little fingers curled around my thumb, and I whispered, *"I love you, Jess."* I kissed her damp, newborn head and held onto that moment for as long as I could.

I promised myself that Jess will have a better life than I had, and I will do whatever it takes to keep her safe and protected. And now, looking at her, I felt that promise was about to shatter.

She looked up at me, her voice barely a whisper. *"Momma, I don't want to play with Daddy anymore."*

A chill ran down my spine. I tried to keep my voice calm. *"What do you mean, Jess?"* She hesitated, then said, *"Daddy touches my private areas ... and he makes me do things I don't like to do. But I don't think it's right, even though he says it's our special thing."*

My stomach twisted. *"He never told me not to tell you"*, she continued, *"but he said you wouldn't understand. He said only daddies and daughters play this game, not mommies and daughters."* She looked up at me, her big brown eyes filling up with tears. *"I just don't want to do it anymore. I don't like it. Can you tell him for me?"*

Her words sent a shiver down my spine. *"If I tell him, I feel like I'll have hell to pay,"* she added softly. I swallowed hard, my voice barely steady. *"What do you mean by that?"* She hesitated, her little fingers twisting together. *"I just know... if I say no, there will be hell to pay. He made that clear."* A storm of emotions raged inside me, but the one that burned the fiercest— was anger. I opened my mouth to speak, but nothing came out.

Not a single word. I was frozen—paralyzed. It felt like someone had punched me in the gut, knocking the wind out of me, leaving me gasping for air. Time stood still. I tried to take a deep breath in. It was painful just to breathe.

Finally, I looked at her, pulling her into my arms. *"I want you to always feel safe with me,"* I whispered, holding her tight. *"You can tell me anything. You don't ever have to be afraid."* Then, I hesitated. My heart pounded in my chest as I forced myself to ask the question. Not because I didn't believe her—I did. But my mind couldn't catch up with the horror of what was happening. *"Are you sure?"*

I needed to hear her say it again. I needed to be absolutely certain before I confronted the monster I had been living with. With hesitancy, she let me know it was the truth. I knew it had taken every ounce of courage for her to tell me that. So, I took a deep breath, hugged her, told her how much I loved her and that everything was going to be ok.

I asked her to wait for me upstairs. She looked terrified, her small frame trembling. *"I'll be right back,"* I promised, though I wasn't sure what was about to happen. I had no idea what I was going to say, but one thing was certain—I refused to look away from the truth. I pushed open the garage door.

The air was thick with smoke, the cigarette scent clinging to everything. It looked like he had gone through an entire pack just within the time I was upstairs. His skin was pale, almost sickly. I sat down beside him, my hands clenched into fists to keep them from shaking.

"Is it true?" I asked, my voice barely above a whisper. He didn't hesitate. "She's lying," he spit on the garage floor then lit another cigarette. "I would never hurt my own flesh and blood. She probably has a boyfriend and is making up some story to keep from getting in trouble."

He took another long drag of his cigarette, his eyes darting away. I glanced down at my own hand—steady no longer, trembling with rage. I hesitated but pulled out a cigarette for myself. I lit it, the flame flickering between us.

Somehow the nicotine seemed to help me gain some composure. *"Is. It. True?" "No,"* he insisted, his voice growing desperate. *"I love you."* I exhaled slowly, the smoke lingering. *"I didn't ask if you loved me. I asked if you touched her."* I turned to face him, my voice ice-cold. *"Is. It. True?"* After he denied it several times, I told him to go upstairs and tell me it wasn't true in front of her.

His face looked like it was two shades of red. He took a deep breath and said, *"let's go"*. At the time, I can't tell you why that seemed like the right thing to do. Looking back, it wasn't. I walked up the stairs first and sat with Jess. He walked up and glared at her. As if she had told his dirty little secret.

I held her next to me. Then I sat down with both of them. I looked at Chris and asked, *"IS IT TRUE?"* He didn't answer. Jess looked at me and said *"yes, it's true"*. He denied it again. Then Jess looked at Chris and said, *"it's true dad, you're lying"*.

Chris stood up and paced the game room for a few seconds. He glared over at Jess again. He finally said it. *"Ok, it IS TRUE... but................ She said it was ok because she knew it was a game."*

I wanted to vomit. I wanted to kill him. I don't remember ever feeling this much anger. But somewhere from the depths of my soul; rage started coming up. All the way to the top and it came out of my mouth.

"IF YOU EVER TOUCH HER AGAIN, I WILL KILL YOU". I had never said those words before. I was shaking as they came out of my mouth. But that day I meant it. I would die protecting Jess; making sure she was safe.

That night, I lay on the couch with Jess curled up beside me, her small body pressed against mine. My mind raced, spinning with guilt and disbelief. How did I not see the signs?

I had convinced myself he was having an affair, but the truth was so much worse. For nine months, he had been molesting our 10-year-old daughter.

How did this happen? I wanted to scream, to release the unbearable weight crushing my chest, but no sound came. My scream was silent, trapped inside me.

Why, God? Why?

Had I missed something? Should I have been looking for signs? But what mother does that? Who suspects something so horrific without reason? I could not stop my tears. My face felt hot and relentless. I wiped them away quickly, as if hiding them could make this nightmare disappear.

A wave of panic lodged itself in my throat, making it hard to breathe. My breath came in shallow gasps. How will Jess heal from this? How will the boys react when they find out their father is a predator? Rage burned through me. I wanted to kill him. I held Jess tight.

She whispered, *"I feel safe with you momma, I feel safe with you."* She snuggled up against me and I felt the tightness in her body begin to relax. I couldn't hold back the tears. I couldn't stop them this time.

I told Jess how much I loved her and how proud I was of her because she was so brave to tell me the truth.

She said, *"All I wanted was for it to stop". I don't hate dad. I just wanted it to stop. It didn't feel right mom, it didn't feel right."*

The next morning, I moved out of my bedroom into Justin's old room. By this time both older boys had moved out and it was only Jeremy, Jess and myself in the house.

I wish I could say I packed up and ran as fast as I could, but fear quickly replaced my anger, and confusion took over my rage. The years of mental and psychological abuse had left me paralyzed. I knew I had to leave—but how?

He knew my every move. He even told me he had people watching, reporting back to him about what I was doing. As the days passed, Chris could sense the shift in the house—he knew he was being watched. But he was a master at twisting reality.

He came to me, pleading for counseling, asking if we could salvage our marriage, reminding me *that divorce was a sin.* As usual, he didn't acknowledge his own sins— only mine. Every single day, he fed me the same lines—how much he regretted what he had done, how he didn't know what he was doing.

He wanted me to think long and hard about leaving him. He reminded me daily that if I asked for a divorce, I would be breaking up our family over something that could easily be "*resolved.*" Resolved? He had to be out of his mind. How could he possibly think we could work this out? How could he believe I could ever love him again, knowing the horror he inflicted on my daughter? I knew I had to get out. But where? Who could I tell? Who would believe me when everyone thought he was the perfect husband? I didn't realize just how deeply the anger had rooted itself inside me.

It had consumed me, tangling itself around every thought. But the worst part was so much of that anger was directed at myself.

I hated that I was afraid to leave. I hated that his threats echoed in my mind, over and over— "If you ever leave me, I will find you". Those words held me captive, keeping me frozen in place when all I wanted was to run.

With everything spiraling out of control, Chris started taking muscle relaxers to help him sleep. Once he slipped into a deep sleep, I would quietly slip into what used to be "our" bedroom and stood beside the bed, just staring at him. I couldn't reconcile how someone I once loved could hurt our daughter. Some nights, I'd watch him sleeping so peacefully and wonder how he could find rest while I was consumed with anger, hatred, and desperate questions to God—how could He let this happen? Eventually, I would turn away and retreat to my own room but sleep never came easily.

My mind was too loud, stuck on the same relentless question: How do I escape?

I didn't just crave justice—I wanted revenge. I wanted him to feel the shame, the pain, and the helplessness that Jess had endured. I needed him to understand what it felt like to be powerless, trapped in fear, just as I did every single day.

Day after day, everything felt mechanical—just going through the motions. I couldn't pretend nothing had happened. I didn't even try to hide my disgust. Every time he walked by me, my skin crawled. Even the scent of his body wash made me physically sick. One weekend, my sister and brother-in-law came to visit, and we all piled into the Suburban. Chris played the role of the doting husband, acting like we were the perfect couple. As if nothing had shattered. As if he wasn't a monster.

At one point, he asked where we wanted to eat, and I turned to look at him. That was it. Just a look. But later, my sister pulled me aside. *"Dude, are you okay?"* she asked, her voice low, serious. *"Yeah, I'm fine. Why?"* She hesitated, then narrowed her eyes. *"Because when you looked at Chris just now... you looked like you wanted to murder him."* Did she just say Murder?

That word reverberated in my head.

My sister was the only one, besides Chris, who truly knew me. If she could read the rage etched across my face—then I had lost control of how much I was showing. My anger, my hatred... was seeping through every crack. And even then, I had to bury it. Hide it. Swallow it whole.

I kept trying to shake off the threats he had made. *"If you ever think about telling anyone what I did, I'll make sure they believe you knew about it—and consented to it. If I go down, you go down with me. They'll take you to jail, and I'll stay with Jess."*

His words haunted me, trapping me in fear. He wanted me to believe there was no escape, that he had all the power. And for a long time, he did. Night after night, those threats kept me awake. The weight of them suffocated me. But after months of praying—pleading—I started finding moments to slip away. I avoided Chris as much as I could, careful to never let my guard down.

The only place I felt even the slightest bit of peace was the garage. It reeked of cigarette smoke, which meant the kids never followed me there. So, I turned it into my sanctuary. My place to pray. My place to plan. My place to hope. Night after night, I paced the garage, praying, pleading, begging God for a way out.

Tears streamed down my face as I wrestled with the silence. Maybe God couldn't hear me. Or worse—maybe He wanted me to stay. Divorce was a sin, wasn't it? Was I meant to endure this? But deep down, I knew—I couldn't stay. Then, one night, after months of unanswered prayers, I reached my breaking point.

I went to the garage like always, but this time, I didn't just whisper. I screamed. "PLEASE, GOD!" My voice echoed off the walls, raw and desperate. "I am afraid to leave. I am afraid of what Chris will do to me. I don't know where to go. I don't know how to escape. I'm terrified he'll find me and kill me if I run. But I know this can't be your plan. Abuse cannot be your plan for us. Is this you will for Jess?

Is this your will for me? Please, God. I need You now more than ever. Help us escape. Help us leave and never look back."

Tears streamed down my face as I knelt on the cold concrete floor, my body aching, my heart heavy, and my hope barely hanging on. I had no more words left to pray. I just sat there in silence, listening to the wind rattling the garage door. And then, in the stillness, I heard it. "Brandy."

I froze. My breath caught in my throat. It was so clear, so real—I thought someone had walked into the garage. I turned around quickly, searching the shadows, but there was no one. Then I heard it again. *"Brandy."* I was too afraid to speak, too afraid to move. My pulse pounded in my ears as I whispered, *"God, what do you mean? What does Brandy mean?"* Silence. And then, one more time. *"Brandy."*

I wiped my tears, my mind racing with questions, and finally forced myself to my feet. Still unsure of what it all meant, I went to bed, wondering what God was trying to tell me.

The next morning, after Chris left for work—now driving over the road for another company—Jess and I headed to the store to pick up a few things. As I parked the car, I pulled out my grocery list, but my mind was elsewhere.

The name I had heard the night before kept replaying in my head. *"Brandy."* What did it mean? Was God trying to tell me something? Was I missing a sign? I couldn't shake the feeling that whatever it was, it was important. We got out of the car and started walking towards the entrance. And out of nowhere, I hear Jess say, "*Mom look*", and walking towards us was "*Brandy*". I couldn't believe it. What is going on?

This is the craziest thing ever.

Brandy was a strong, beautiful and unapologetic woman who served in the Booster Club with Chris. He didn't like her because she was "opinionated", and she wasn't afraid to speak the truth. They had worked together on some projects and that year it was for the senior class of 2011.

There was one time Brandy came over to the house to work on something with Chris. I can't even remember what it was, but I gave my input on it. I liked Brandy's idea, but something was said that set Chris off. His frustration quickly turned into anger, and before I knew it, he was degrading me—right in front of her. I felt my face burn with embarrassment, but I didn't say a word.

Chris stormed out the back door to smoke a cigarette. Brandy sat down next to me on the couch, her eyes kind and full of concern. *"He shouldn't be treating you like that,"* she said softly.

I'm sure she said more, but by then, I had already shut down. Like always, I made an excuse for him. Something about him being frustrated, how this was just the way he was. The usual *blah blah blah* I told myself to justify his behavior. The truth was, I had been degraded so often that I barely reacted anymore.

I had become numb to it. Numb to everything. Brandy never hesitated to tell Chris the truth, and she wasn't afraid to challenge him. I admired that about her. She had a strength I wished I had. Every time she disagreed with him, I silently cheered her on, imagining what it would feel like if that were me—if I could be that brave. After that *incident*, Chris made it clear that I was never to speak to Brandy again.

I wasn't surprised. That was his pattern—anyone who stood against him, he cut off. And that meant they were cut off from my life too. He was angry at the whole world, and since I lived in *his* world, I was trapped inside it. It felt like suffocating in an airtight bubble with no way out.

Weeks passed, but I couldn't stop thinking about that chance encounter with Brandy in the Walmart parking lot.

"It felt like more than a coincidence—it felt like a divine appointment. Before she left, she had looked me in the eyes and said, *"If you ever need anything, don't hesitate to call me"*. I thought about those words over and over. Then one day, Jess came to me and said *"Mom, maybe we should go see Brandy?"*

I wanted to go. I needed to go. But fear kept its grip on me. Chris always told me he had eyes everywhere—that he could find out anything I did just by asking around. I even convinced myself that he had hidden cameras in the house, listening, watching. I lived in a constant state of fear and paranoia.

It took everything in me to finally call Brandy. Even as I dialed her number, I was certain Chris had tapped my phone, that he would somehow *know*. Brandy invited us over for dinner while Chris was out of town. The entire drive there, my hands were shaking on the steering wheel. When we pulled into her driveway, I hesitated, my heart pounding. I scanned the street—left, then right. Was anyone watching? Was Chris going to call me any second, demanding to know where I was?

Jess and I hurried inside, shutting the door behind us. I exhaled a breath I didn't even realize I was holding. We made small talk, but I kept glancing at the door, expecting to hear a knock at any moment. Expecting him to find me.

As we talked, a sick feeling churned in my stomach. It felt like I was about to vomit. My hands were clammy, my heart raced. Then, before I could stop myself, the words came spilling out—fast and frantic, as if saying them quickly would somehow keep Chris from hearing. Maybe if I got it out fast enough, even his imaginary recording devices wouldn't catch it.

The moment the words left my lips, the weight of it all crashed down on me. I broke. Not just tears—*a wailing cry* from deep inside, a sound I didn't even recognize as my own. It was raw, years of pain and fear finally escaping. Then Jess cried too. Brandy sat there, stunned at first. But within seconds, she pulled herself together like she *knew* what had to happen next.

Meanwhile, I was still sobbing, caught between the relief of finally speaking the truth and the terror of what came next. Chris is going to kill me. The thought looped in my mind.

I could almost see him storming up to Brandy's house, yanking me out the door. Brandy met my eyes, steady and unwavering.

"We need a plan," she said. "It's time for you to leave." And in that moment, the pieces finally clicked.

Brandy.

She was the answer to my desperate prayers. God was using her to help me escape. But I knew... we still had a long road ahead.

Courage- The ability to control your fear in a dangerous or difficult situation~ Cambridge Dictionary

For God did not give us a spirit of timidity or cowardice or fear, but [He has given us a spirit] of power and of love and of sound judgment and personal discipline [abilities that result in a calm, well-balanced mind and self-control] 2 Timothy 1:7.-Amplified Bible

I left Brandy's house with a big sense of relief but also an extra layer of anxiety. The secret was out, and we had no time to waste. I didn't know the first thing about escaping my home, but at this point, I knew if I left, he would find me. That is something Chris reminded me of often. And when he did find me, there would be hell to pay.

I believed him. I knew he was capable of all the threats he'd made over the years. The thing about mental abuse is you believe everything they tell you, even if you know it's not true. They could say the sky is green but even if you look up and see the sky is clearly blue, you will believe it's green. I lived in a mental prison of fear, and I didn't know how to get out. The anger and rage were now a puddle of anxiety and fear. I had no idea how to plan an escape, so I turned to Google, searching frantically for answers—child molestation, sexual abuse, how to get help. There was an overwhelming amount of information for counseling, but nothing that told me exactly who to ask for help.

Then the questions started creeping in, twisting my thoughts into knots.

What if I stayed? Would he keep his hands off her? What if he went to counseling—would the counselor report him? What if I left too soon? What if he actually got help? What if I had nowhere to go? What if we ended up on the streets? What if... what if I had just let him keep abusing me instead? Would that have kept him away from Jess? The thoughts sickened me, but they wouldn't stop. I was drowning in uncertainty, torn between fear, guilt, and the desperate need to escape. I couldn't hold it in any longer. The weight of what he had done to her— especially after she described it in painful detail—made me sick to my stomach. I wanted him to suffer. I wanted him to feel every ounce of pain he had inflicted on us. The years of abuse, the way he treated the boys, and now this? It was too much.

But I couldn't scream. I didn't want anyone to hear me.

So, alone in my room, staring at the same wall for hours, I opened my mouth and screamed—silently.

It became my ritual. No sound came out, but in my mind, I was standing in a vast, empty field. No one around. Just me, God, and endless open space.

There, I screamed as loud as my lungs would allow, until my throat felt raw. I screamed out all the pain, the guilt, the unbearable shame. I screamed because I didn't see the signs. I screamed because I wasn't there to protect her. And then, just like that, I was back in my room. Still staring at the wall. Still silent. After hours of research, I finally found some useful information. If we left, we couldn't keep our current phone lines—he could track us.

That was the first step. I applied for a new phone plan and was approved for three lines. I could hardly believe it. It felt like a small victory, a confirmation that God was guiding me, even if I was taking baby steps. When placing the order, I made sure to request that no receipts or contract information be mailed to our address.

Unfortunately, the phones had to be delivered there—I couldn't find a way around it. The woman on the phone reassured me that all billing and contract details would be sent to my email instead. The phones would arrive in three to five days. I prayed Chris would be out of town when they did. But then, as always, the doubts came flooding in. *"I can't leave. Who am I kidding?" "Chris said I'd never make it without him." "He said I'd end up in a dangerous neighborhood, robbed and struggling." "No one will ever want me—with four kids." "He's the only one who could ever love me." "Other men might try, but no one could love me like he does." "How could I possibly take care of myself and the kids?"*

The words he had drilled into me over the years echoed in my mind, trying to keep me trapped. Around that time, as I sat lost in my thoughts, Jeremy arrived home from school. He already knew what had happened to Jess.

We had been through what Chris dismissively called an "incident." Someone had anonymously reported him to CPS, launching an investigation. We were told a caseworker would be coming by the house to speak with us in a few days. When Chris got home, we had no choice but to tell him. The moment the words left my mouth, his face twisted with rage. Without saying a word, he stormed upstairs and barged into Jess's room without knocking. Then came the yelling—furious, venomous. My heart pounded.

I sprinted up the stairs, desperate to get to her. Chris was in Jess's face, screaming at the top of his lungs. *"Do you know what you just did? You just opened a HUGE can of worms. I hope you're proud of yourself."* But he didn't stop there. By the time I reached Jess's room, he had already lunged at her. Instinct took over—I stepped in between them. He shoved me aside like I was nothing and slammed Jess against the wall, hurling profanities at her. Without thinking, I pushed him back, but before I could react, I was on the floor. Chris was on top of me, his hands around my throat.

I should have felt pain. I should have felt terror. But instead, there was this strange sense of calm. It was like an invisible shield had wrapped around me. I could see his hands squeezing, but I felt nothing. Then, out of nowhere, a blur of movement flashed over me. It was Jeremy. He launched himself at his father, tackling him to the ground.

Jeremy had been on the wrestling team at school, and in that moment, every bit of his training kicked in. He pinned Chris down, his voice shaking with rage. "*You better calm your ass down, or I will hurt you,*" Jeremy yelled, trying to get Chris' to stop lunging at me and Jess.

I turned to look at my son. His eyes burned with fury, years of pain and resentment boiling over. He had Chris locked in a chokehold, unrelenting. "*Are you settled down now?*" Jeremy shouted again. Chris gasped for air, his face turning pale. "*Stop—please—I think I'm going to have a heart attack. Let me go. I can't breathe.*" I watched as the color drained from his face. Then, just before it was too late, Jeremy released him. Jeremy—barely a hundred and twenty-five pounds soaking wet—had just taken down Chris, a man twice his size. Chris caught his breath, then staggered into the bedroom and shut the door behind him.

He didn't come out for the rest of the night. Downstairs, I found Jeremy sitting motionless, staring into space. He looked lost, his mind somewhere far away. I leaned in gently asked- "*Are you okay?*" He snapped. "*NO, MOM! I'M NOT OKAY! I COULD HAVE KILLED MY DAD!*" His voice shook with a mixture of rage and disbelief.

The weight of what had just happened crashed down on both of us. It's incredible what the mind does to protect itself from trauma —but at that moment, there was no blocking it out. I wrapped my arms around him, but he didn't hug me back. I held on anyway. "*I love you, Jeremy, I know you're angry, and I know this is too much*" I whispered. "*But you are going to be okay. And somehow, we are getting out of here.*" His body went limp in my arms, like all the fight had drained out of him. And then he broke. Tears spilled down his face as his body shook with sobs.

By then, Jess had joined us. She wrapped her arms around Jeremy, and together, we cried—years of fear and pain pouring out in silence. After a while, Jeremy wiped his face and looked at us. *"Are y'all okay?"* Jess and I nodded-*"Scared, but okay."* Jess hugged him tightly. *"Thank you."* That night, Jeremy slept on one couch, and Jess and I curled up on the other. None of us truly slept.

We kept one eye open, waiting, unsure of what would come next. The next morning, Chris walked downstairs and casually headed to the kitchen to make coffee, as if nothing had happened the night before. My heart pounded. I had no idea what to expect—another outburst? More threats? Jeremy sat at the table, quietly eating his cereal, his face unreadable. Chris chuckled. *"Wow, Jeremy, I didn't know you were that strong," he said, stirring his coffee. "Remind me never to get you mad."* He laughed again, like it was all some kind of joke, then turned and walked back upstairs.

I stood there, frozen. Stunned. He wasn't remorseful. He wasn't ashamed. He wasn't even angry. To him, last night's violence was nothing more than a punchline of his sick joke. Throughout the day, he kept making jokes about it, laughing as he teased Jeremy about "flying through the air like a lemur." I watched Jeremy's jaw clench every time Chris spoke. He didn't respond. He just sat there, absorbing every word. But I could see it in his eyes—he wasn't going to forget. Neither would I. A few days after the brutal fight, I came home exhausted from work, just wanting to crawl into bed.

As I dragged myself to the bathroom, I moved cautiously, hoping to avoid Chris. But before I could close the door behind me, he was there.

He stepped inside and shut the door. For a long moment, he just stared at me—silent, unmoving. The air felt thick, suffocating. My pulse pounded as I glanced at the door, calculating an escape. "I need to shower," my voice was shaky- "*Can you leave*?" Still, he said nothing. The silence stretched unbearably, pressing in on me like a weight I couldn't shake.

Then finally, his eyes hardened, and in a low, controlled voice, he said, "*Make this go away.*"

My stomach twisted. "*You and Jess put me in this situation*," he continued, his words slow, deliberate, laced with quiet rage. "*So, you are going to do whatever it takes to fix it. Do you understand?*" I swallowed hard, trapped between the sink and the monster I once called my husband.

I didn't respond. I just stood there, frozen, my mind racing. How was I supposed to make this go away? I knew exactly what he meant. He was talking about the CPS visit we were about to walk into. After my shower, I dressed quickly and made my way downstairs, my heart pounding. Jess was sitting on the couch, and I sat beside her. Chris followed, lowering himself into the chair across from us, his eyes cold and unblinking. His glare bore into us, making it clear—we were under his control. Fear wrapped itself around us like a vice.

I had no idea what to say to the CPS worker. No idea how to navigate the impossible. If I told the truth, would they arrest me and leave Jess with him? Would they think I had been hiding it? I wasn't hiding anything—I was just trying to keep us alive. They had no idea of the daily threats. The constant bullying. The invisible chains that held us prisoners in our own home. He leaned in closer, his voice low and eerily calm.

It didn't sound right—too controlled, too cold.

"This is your mess to clean up," he murmured. "You made it. Now fix it... or else. The words sent a chill down my spine. A short while later, the CPS investigator arrived. Chris, always the performer, put on his Coach's T-shirt, the only season he'd helped out when Jess played softball. The mask was on. The show was about to begin.

Every picture on the wall was framed in the same color, evenly spaced, perfectly aligned, nothing out of place. A reflection of the illusion Chris had so carefully constructed. As he descended the stairs to answer the door, he shot a look at Jess and me. A silent warning. His stare was sharp, calculated, a reminder that at any moment, he could snap—and we would be the ones to pay. Then, in an instant, the mask slipped into place.

He pulled the door open, flashing a wide, welcoming smile. *"Hi there! My name is Chris. This is my beautiful wife, Chrissie, and our daughter, Jessika. Please, come in."* His voice was warm, inviting—so convincing it made my stomach turn. The investigator stepped inside, immediately greeted by walls filled with carefully curated family photos and collages. A perfect façade of love and happiness. I clenched my hands to keep steady, swallowing the nausea rising in my throat. Chris was playing the role of a doting husband and devoted father. And I had no choice but to sit through the performance.

The investigator smiled as he glanced around the room. "*You have such a beautiful family,*" he commented. Chris, being the performer he was, leaned closer to me, his hand resting on mine as if we were the picture-perfect couple. I hoped—prayed—that the investigator would see through it.

That he would notice how forced it all was. That he'd think, He's acting too nice. He must be hiding something. But that's not what happened. Chris offered him a glass of water—polite, hospitable, calculated. The investigator declined, and we all sat down at the kitchen table. With a professional but firm tone, he began, *"We received an anonymous allegation of sexual molestation. We take these claims very seriously, and our goal is to rule out any false accusations."* Chris didn't flinch. *"Absolutely. We'll tell you whatever you need to know,"* he said smoothly. *"We have nothing to hide."*

I turned to look at him, and for the first time, I realized—I had no idea who I was married to anymore. My heart pounded in my chest as a thought crept in. *"Maybe I can tell the investigator. Maybe he can help us"*. The investigator explained that he would need to speak with each of us separately. Chris's expression shifted—a surprised look came across his face before he quickly masked it.

I could see his hands twitching slightly as he leaned forward. "Wouldn't it be better if we all stayed together?" he suggested with, a nervous tone in his voice. "That way, we can all hear what's being said. Total transparency."

*T*he investigator offered a polite but firm smile. *"I understand your concern, Mr. Moore, but that's not how we conduct our interviews. We'll start with you. Where would you like to talk?"*

"The garage will work." Chris hesitated for a split second before nodding. As he stood, he walked over to me, pressing a kiss to my forehead. *"I'll be right back, babe. It'll be okay,"* he murmured.

Then, he took my hand and squeezed it—not a reassuring loving squeeze, but a silent warning. A reminder. Remember what I told you. After speaking with Chris, it was my turn, then Jess. When he had finished with Jess, he smiled and asked if there had been any disagreements with friends of the family lately.

We told him we weren't aware of any. He explained that sometimes when a relationship dissolves, there tends to be disgruntled parties. He explained that he truly believed someone had a grudge against us. This intrigued Chris so he asked the investigator if he could tell us who made the allegations. The investigator couldn't give us any names, but he did say *"The caller seemed so convincing on the phone. She was so worried about your daughter. Don't worry, Mr. Moore, from what I can see here, you have a fine home. You seem to have a beautiful family and sometimes others can be jealous of what others have."*

He told us he'd be in touch within a few days, but he didn't feel there was anything to report here. He shook our hands and walked out. Chris waited for the investigator to walk to his car. He opened the door and drove away.

Chris looked at me with a smug grin and said, *"And that's how it's done."* Then he turned and stomped upstairs, slamming the door behind him. We had lied. Out of fear, out of desperation. We were too afraid to tell the truth, terrified of what he might do if we did.

The threats, the control was all too much. He had manipulated us into protecting him. I wish I could say I ran after the investigator's car, that he stopped, turned around, and saved us. But that didn't happen. If he could convince a CPS investigator, how would anyone ever believe me? A few days later, the call came; case closed.

Chris smirked. *"You can't leave now,"* he sneered. *"Because if I go down, you go down with me."* With everything that had happened, I felt completely trapped—like there was no way out.

But deep down, I kept hoping; kept searching for a way to escape.

Several months had passed, and I was still in a fog. I moved through my days, functioning but disconnected. By then, I was working for an airline and my shift started at 6 a.m. I had to leave for work before Jess left to school and the thought of her being alone with Chris worried me.

To ease my anxiety, I asked Jess to keep me on her cell phone while she was getting ready. She would explain; "Now I'm drying my hair. Now I'm walking out of the house. Now I'm at the bus stop, etc."

I couldn't be there with her, but in some small way, she carried me along until she was safely on the bus. One morning, Chris tried to convince Jess to stay home from school. *"It's a beautiful day,"* he said. *"We can hang out by the pool. I'll put some tanning lotion on you, so you don't burn."* Jess shut him down immediately. *"No. I'm not skipping school, and I don't want to go to the pool with you."* His face darkened with anger.

Without another word, he went back upstairs. When he came back down, his expression was cold. "*Well, then,*" he said. "*You'll have to figure out a way to school on your own—because I'm not taking you.*" I'm not sure why he acted like her only option was for him to take her —he hadn't driven her to school in months. Jess, relieved, shrugged and said, *"I don't care, I'll ride the bus."* She slammed the front door behind her and ran toward the bus stop.

But Chris wasn't done. He got into his truck and followed her. When he pulled up beside her, he ordered her to get in. She hesitated but, knowing better than to resist, she climbed in and sat stiffly in the front seat of his truck.

He stared at her, his voice low and cold. *"This is your fault, you know,"* he said. *"Because you told your mom what happened, now there's a wedge between us."* He paused, then added cruelly, *"You wanted me to do it. You never said no."* Jess jumped out of the truck and onto the bus without looking back.

The moment she found a seat, she called me, her sobs so heavy I could barely understand her words.

"Mom, I never want to go back home again." Panic surged through me. Without hesitation, I left work. My job was an hour away, but I drove as fast as I could, my hands gripping the wheel, my heart pounding. By the time I reached the house, Chris had already gone —off to work, out of town. I collapsed onto the couch and sat there for hours, lost in a fog of fear and exhaustion. Jess was safe at school, but I felt anything but safe. The tears came hard and didn't stop.

Eventually, I dragged myself upstairs and sat on the edge of my bed, staring out the window. Below, the world carried on as if nothing had happened. The hiking trails stretched along the landscape, a gentle stream glistened in the sunlight, a mother pushed her baby in a stroller. Laughter rang out from a group of kids playing ball, their joy so effortless, so free. I watched them feeling numb thinking *"How did I end up here?"* After a while, I heard footsteps coming up the stairs. It was Jeremy—home early from school.

He stepped into my room and saw me sitting there, staring blankly out the window. Without hesitation, he wrapped his arms around me. "*Mom, we have to leave. We have to get out of here,*" he said, his voice firm but pleading. *"I know you're scared, but we can't stay here anymore."* Before I could respond, the garage door opened. The sound sent a jolt through my body. I froze. Panic gripped me like a vice. I wanted to move, to run—but my feet felt cemented to the floor. I held my breath while fear gripped my mind. Chris was home. And he was going to be furious. Jeremy saw it in my face.

He felt it in the air. He knew. The garage door opened and shut. Jeremy tensed. *"Mom, stay here."*

"Don't move. I'll go see if it's Dad." He stepped toward the stairs and called out, *"Who's here?"* Silence. He called again, louder this time. *"Who's here?"* Then, finally, Jess's voice rang out. *"It's me, Jeremy."* Jess had arrived from school. Relief flooded through me. I hadn't even realized I was holding my breath until I exhaled all at once. Jeremy turned back to me; his eyes locked onto mine. *"Mom, look at me. We have to go. Now. Today."*

I couldn't move. It was as if invisible weights were strapped to my ankles, holding me in place. Jeremy stepped closer, urgency in his voice. *"Mom, we have to get out of here NOW."* I turned, my eyes darting around the room.

A wave of confusion washed over me. My mind splintered into a thousand thoughts. Where do I even start? What do I pack? Do I take the kids' baby pictures? How can I grab everything I need in just minutes? Do I leave behind the boxes and boxes of memories? Where do I put my clothes? Chris could walk through that door at any second. There was no time. I took a deep breath, grabbed a trash bag, and started stuffing things inside– blindly, frantically. I didn't even look at what I was taking. All I could think about was how my entire life was being crammed into a single trash bag. I couldn't think. I just kept crying and crying. Mostly out of fear.

Why me, Lord? Why is this happening to me? I called Brandy, and she came over right away. Everything I could fit—was stuffed into a single black trash bag. Except for the guns. We took those. A 12-gauge, a 20-gauge, and a handgun. I didn't want to take any chances that Chris would get them and use them on us. Everything was left behind. When I say we left with nothing but the clothes on our backs, I mean exactly that. Just what we were wearing and whatever we could cram into that bag.

The emotions crashed over me like a tidal wave. The panic of sneaking out, the gut-wrenching reality of leaving behind everything I had worked so hard for. It wasn't fair. He got to stay. I hated him for putting us in this nightmare. Brandy was going to drive us to a domestic violence shelter in downtown Fort Worth. Before we left, I turned to her, my voice shaking. *"Can you please take care of my dogs?"*

I had three—my German Shepherd, my Lab, and my little Weenie dog. It hadn't even crossed my mind until that moment, where they were going to go? I couldn't bear the thought of them ending up in a shelter, only to be euthanized. As if everything else wasn't already unbearable, now I had to let go of them too. My heart shattered. Brandy must have seen the sheer panic in my eyes. She grabbed my hand firmly and said, *"Chrissie, you're coming to my house. You, Jeremy, Jess, and all three dogs—let's go."* I broke down, wrapping my arms around her, sobbing into her shoulder.

Relief. Fear. Gratitude. It all hit me at once. I had already gotten my new phones, and fortunately when they arrived, Justin was at the house, so he hid them in my closet. so, I left my old ones on the counter.

Next to them, on a plain white piece of paper, I wrote: "**I left. Do not come find me. I am safe. The kids are safe. Go get help**." And with that, I walked out the door. That was the day I escaped. A heavy cloud of fear wrapped around me, suffocating and inescapable. *"Just keep going, Chrissie. Just keep going."* I forced one foot in front of the other and climbed into the car. My hands trembled. My heart pounded so hard I could hear it in my ears. Every breath felt shallow, like I couldn't get enough air. Gripping the steering wheel tightly, I tried to steady myself, but the shaking wouldn't stop.

My eyes darted everywhere, convinced Chris could see me— like there was some hidden camera recording my every move. The knots in my stomach tightened. Still gripped by the fear that Chris had someone watching me, I carefully, almost silently, clicked my seatbelt into place. *Click.* The sound echoed in my ears, too loud, too final. I shifted the car into drive, but my foot refused to press the gas.

Fear took over, locking me in place. I glanced in the rearview mirror. *"I never said goodbye".* Another wave of emotion crashed over me. I knew I would never see him again. I knew that if I turned back now, I'd never escape. I'd be trapped forever. Tears blurred my vision as I gripped the steering wheel and whispered into the silence, *"Why, God? Why did this happen to us?* I was a good wife. I did everything I was supposed to do. I kept driving, but a flood of emotions crashed over me, each one heavier than the last. I had finally found the courage to escape, yet all I felt was guilt.

I thought I would feel relieved, maybe even free—but instead, I felt lost. Despite everything we had endured, a voice in my head kept whispering, *"Am I doing the right thing?" "Did I give up too soon?"*

The LORD is close to the brokenhearted and saves those who are crushed in spirit. Psalm 34:18 NIV

When I arrived at Brandy's house, it was difficult to unwind. The lingering fear that Chris might show up at any moment kept me on edge. As the night wore on, exhaustion took over, leaving me with little energy to fight it. In a way, we were "in hiding," and the weight of it all was overwhelming. Jess, Daisy (our German Shepherd), and I settled into one room, while Jeremy slept in the other with Marley and Weenie.

For the first time in what felt like forever, I slept through the entire night. I woke up the next morning, surprised that I had actually gotten a full night's rest. But within minutes, the reality of my situation hit me like a wave. This wasn't a dream. It was real. I had left.

I had escaped. Determined to maintain a sense of normalcy, especially for Jeremy and Jess, I stuck to our usual routine, hoping it would keep our minds occupied. I dropped the kids off at school, but my senses were heightened—I found myself scanning my surroundings more than usual.

Even though Chris was out of town, I couldn't shake the fear that he might show up at any moment. What I didn't realize was that Jess had already confided in her coach about everything that had been happening. The coach was legally required to report the situation, which meant we once again found ourselves meeting with CPS.

Brandy suggested that I consider getting a restraining order to protect our safety. It wasn't something I wanted to do, but deep down, I knew it was the right decision. She drove me to the Benbrook Police Department, where I reluctantly explained everything to an officer.

He was kind and listened attentively, but after I finished, he gently informed me that because I technically lived in Fort Worth, I would need to go to a Fort Worth police station to file the report. A wave of relief washed over me—deep down, I didn't want to report Chris to the police.

I just wanted the pain to stop and to make sure Jess was safe. The thought of telling anyone terrified me. It had taken me this long just to confide in Brandy—how was I supposed to explain everything to the police?

We had escaped. We were alive. Couldn't we just move on? Still, we drove to another police department. As we walked in, Brandy asked if we could speak with a detective. While we waited, fear crept in. Where would we even begin?

How could we possibly explain everything—years of mental and sexual abuse? Jess turned to me, her voice trembling. *"Momma, I'm scared. What if Dad finds out we came here? Won't he be super mad at us?"*

Before I could respond, a detective stepped out and introduced himself. He explained that in order to file for a restraining order, he needed details about what was happening. I took a deep breath and began recounting the abuse—how afraid we were, how long it had been going on.

I tried to stay composed, but my voice trembled, and I kept glancing at the small window in the door, half-expecting Chris to somehow find out I was there. Then, the detective said something that left me speechless. *"So, let me get this straight—you're telling me your husband has been abusing you and is now abusing your daughter, but you couldn't pick up the phone and call 911? How hard is it to pick up the phone?"*

Shock paralyzed me. My mind raced, searching for the right words. "I was afraid," I finally managed to say. "You don't understand—he would have killed me or killed us."

Tears welled up in my eyes as I tried to explain, but the more I spoke, the more my thoughts tangled, my words stumbling over each other. I wanted him to see—*really* see—how trapped

I had been. But all I felt was judgment. He told me that by staying in the house, knowing what had happened to my daughter, I was guilty of Child Endangerment—and that I could go to jail. *"Me? Go to jail?"*

My mind reeled. "*What about what Chris did?"* So, after all the fear, all the pain, and after finally risking my life to escape, I was the one who might end up behind bars? I felt myself sinking into the chair, my body growing smaller under the weight of his words.

Had I made a terrible mistake? Should I have just stayed? If Chris found out about this, he *would* kill me—I was sure of it. The detective turned his attention to Jess, asking her questions. I could see her body tensing, her fingers gripping the sides of her chair.

She kept glancing at me, fear in her eyes. "*Don't look at your mom,"* he said sharply. "*Just answer the question."* That was it. I couldn't do this. "*I think we better leave,"* I said, standing abruptly. I took Jess by the hand, and we rushed out of the lobby, straight to where Brandy was waiting.

Tears streamed down my face as I pleaded with her. *"I knew we shouldn't have come here. Please, take me back to your house. I can't do this, I'm too scared."* Brandy's face hardened. *"What did he say to you?"*

Through my sobs, I tried to explain, my words tumbling over each other. But she heard *enough.* Without hesitation, she spun around, marched up to the front counter, and demanded to speak to the detective.

I couldn't quite hear the whole thing, but I do know she told them *"Do you even know how hard it was to get them here?" "Find me someone else they can talk to"* she insisted. It felt like I was the one in trouble. I could hear Brandy raising her voice then quietly sat next to me and hugged me. She said *"they are going to find someone else, don't leave just yet. You have to let them know what happened to you and Jess".*

After about 45 minutes of waiting, we finally got to speak with someone else.

Before I go into this next part of my story, the timeline of the meetings with CPS as well as the police investigation are still to this day hard for me to remember. I will do my best to bring the most accurate accounts of what happened.*

Since Jess had confided in her coach at school, he was legally required to report what she had shared. The school then contacted CPS. By that time, we had already escaped and were hiding at Brandy's house.

We went to the police department to report the abuse and request a protective order to ensure Chris couldn't come near me or the kids —even at their school. When the second detective came to speak with us, we finally had the chance to explain everything. This time, we felt a little less afraid as we shared our story.

A few days after going to the police, I was contacted by the school counselor. We met in her office, where she explained that she had spoken with Jess. She assured me that despite everything Jess had endured, her grades and participation at school remained unaffected.

"She's a very strong and brave girl," the counselor told me, but then added something that unsettled me. *"In cases like this, girls tend to go one of two ways. They either become extremely promiscuous, or they never want to be in a relationship with* a man."
I sat there, trying to process what she had just said. Were those really the only two paths my daughter had? I thanked her for reaching out, but in my heart, I rejected that notion.

In Jesus' name, those will not be the only choices for my daughter.
With a new case now open, the investigation turned toward both Jess and me. They took Jess into another room while I remained with the detective and the CPS investigator.

After a few minutes, they both left the room to interview her, leaving me alone with my thoughts, anxiously waiting for what would come next.

That same week, after speaking with the counselor, I was asked to return to the police department with Jess to provide a detailed account of what had happened. What I didn't realize was that the CPS investigator would also be present.

Before that meeting, I confided in Brandy, sharing what the detective had told me during my last visit—that I could face jail time for "Child Endangerment" because I had stayed in the home despite knowing about the previous abuse.

Deep down, I knew the detective wasn't wrong. But all I could think about was how terrified I had been. I wished people could truly understand the kind of fear that paralyzes you when you're told you'll be killed if you ever leave.

Still, if going to jail meant Jess would be safe, then so be it. At least he could never hurt her again. With that thought weighing on me, I asked Brandy a question I never imagined I'd have to ask—one she had every reason to say no to.

We weren't related, and she had already raised her two daughters. *"If I go to jail,"* I said, my voice shaking, *"could you please take care of Jess until I get out?"* I knew Jeremy would be heading off to college soon, living in the dorms. But Jess... she still needed someone.

I needed to know she would be loved and protected. I couldn't stop thinking about our conversation. In my mind, I was already preparing for the possibility of being prosecuted. I was bracing myself to go to jail. In some ways, I had been living in a prison all along—the only difference was that this one would have real bars.

The home I had lived in for years had invisible ones. The day of the interview, the detective led us into a room. Jess was taken to another room where she would have to answer painful, difficult questions while they recorded her testimony. I wasn't allowed to be with her. It felt like I waited for hours.

I tried not to picture what they were asking her, but my heart ached knowing she was being forced to relive every awful detail. I stared at the floor, trying to silence the thoughts racing through my mind. But no matter how hard I tried, one phrase kept replaying over and over—Chris' chilling words:

"If you ever leave me, I will find you."

As I sat alone in that empty room, the weight of regret crushed me. I replayed every decision, every moment that led us here. If only I had left sooner, Jess wouldn't have suffered. If only I had found the courage to escape, we wouldn't be in this position.

If only I had seen the red flags when I met him, I would have never married him. My mind spiraled, flashing through the future I feared losing—missing my grandchildren grow up, missing Christmases, birthdays, maybe even weddings. My heart ached with the unbearable thought of it all.

Then, the door creaked open, snapping me out of my thoughts. Jess' interview was over. Now, it was my turn. I felt like a criminal. Fear gripped me as I clutched the wooden chair beneath my hands. My voice barely escaped as I muttered, "Is Jess okay?" A brief silence filled the room before the detective met my eyes.

"Your daughter is very brave," he said. "She gave us detailed accounts of the abuse."

Tears streamed down my face. I could only imagine the pain of her having to relive those horrors, to put words to things no child should ever have to say. Then, the detective's next words changed everything. "Mrs. Moore, your husband has so many counts against him... he's going to prison for a very long time."

Tears poured down my face as I struggled to breathe. It felt like an elephant was sitting on my chest, crushing every ounce of air from my lungs. No matter how hard I tried, I couldn't take a full breath. The detective sat in silence, watching me. His gaze felt heavy, filled with judgment. Shame wrapped around me like a suffocating blanket. I wanted to disappear, to shrink into nothing. I wanted to be anywhere but in that room.

For a fleeting moment, I wished I didn't exist at all. The CPS investigator was there too. Her voice broke through the fog of my panic.

"Jess was very brave," she said gently. I couldn't look at her. My eyes stayed locked on the floor as if looking up would make everything even more real. Then, she asked me a question. *"Mrs. Moore, do you know how many people lie to CPS every year?"*

My voice was barely a whisper. *"No, I don't."* The words caught in my throat, strangled by the sobs I couldn't control. I swallowed hard, desperately trying to hold myself together. The CPS investigator continued, her voice steady yet firm.

"Hundreds of people," she said. "Do you know why?" I shook my head, barely able to form words. *"I don't know why"* I answered. *"Because they're afraid,"* she explained. *"Afraid to tell the truth out of fear their abuser will kill them."*

Her words cut through me like a blade, exposing the fear I had carried for so long. She took a deep breath before continuing. *"We spoke with Jessika, and like we said before, she's incredibly brave."*

Then she paused, her expression softening. *"After Jessika told us everything, she asked us for something."* My heart pounded as I waited for her to continue. She said, *"Please don't take my mom away from me. She's the only one I feel safe with. It isn't her fault. We were both scared he would hurt us. Please don't take my mom away from me.'"*

Tears welled in my eyes again, but this time, they weren't just from fear— they were from the weight of my daughter's love and courage. I lost control. They handed me a tissue, but it did little to stop the flood of emotions that had been buried deep for so long. No matter how hard I tried to keep it together, the pain refused to stay hidden. It poured out of me, raw and relentless.

The detective studied me for a moment before speaking. *"Mrs. Moore, you're going to have to live with the decision you made to stay in that home for the rest of your life."* As if I didn't already know that. As if I hadn't spent every sleepless night drowning in guilt, blaming myself for not leaving sooner.

His words weren't necessary—I had already sentenced myself to a lifetime of regret. I braced myself for what was coming next. Just say it. Just arrest me already. The waiting was unbearable. I was ready to accept whatever punishment they had for me—I just needed to see Jess one last time. I needed to hug her; to tell her how much I loved her, to remind her that she would always be my reason why.

The CPS investigator's voice finally broke the silence. *"Mrs. Moore, based on the accounts Jessika has given us, we are choosing not to press any charges. Since you've removed yourselves from the home, she is no longer in immediate danger. And we understand why you were too afraid to speak out before."*

She looked me in the eyes.

"You are free to take your daughter and go."

I collapsed to the floor, overcome with a mix of agony and relief so intense that my body couldn't hold it in. I sobbed uncontrollably, unable to move, as the weight of everything crashed over me. Then, they let Jess into the room. The moment I saw her, I pulled her into my arms, holding her tightly. *"I'm not going to jail,"* I whispered through my tears. Jess looked up at me, her voice steady and sure. *"I know, Momma. I'm going to be safe with you."*

The detective gave me a moment before explaining the next step. He told me that he would be calling Chris—it was standard protocol. To avoid raising suspicion, he planned to tell Chris that someone had reported the abuse, and before moving forward, they wanted to hear his side of the story.

An appointment was set for May 22nd in the afternoon. The exact time was uncertain since Chris hadn't been returning the detective's calls. But it was only a matter of time. We left the station, and Brandy drove us back to her house.

The moment we pulled into the driveway, my heart dropped. There, taped to my car window, was a 5x7 manila envelope. I froze, my stomach twisting into knots. “He found us,” I whispered to myself. “Just like he said he would”

My hands trembled as I reached for the envelope, struggling to peel the tape away. When I finally managed to open it, I pulled out a folded piece of notebook paper with a receipt from the Academy taped to it.

My breath hitched as I sifted through the contents—several of our wedding photos. At the top of the paper, written in bold letters, were the words: "TILL DEATH DO US PART." My eyes darted to the receipt. My blood ran cold. A 9mm handgun. We had made sure to take our shotguns and handgun when we left, knowing we couldn’t risk leaving any weapons in the house. But now, he had another one.

My vision blurred, but all I could see—over and over again—were those haunting words: "TILL DEATH DO US PART." We reported the incident to the police department. At the time, my oldest son, Justin, was working with Chris.

They drove together as co-drivers for a trucking contractor, spending long hours on the road together. In the weeks leading up to our escape, Justin would call me in tears, feeling like he was losing his mind. Chris was manipulating him—twisting reality, making him believe that Jess was lying about the abuse.

According to Chris, her so-called "lies" were the reason our marriage had fallen apart. Justin was caught in an emotional storm. One minute, Chris would break down, confessing that he had done it, apologizing through his sobs. The next, he would turn cold, cursing me and Jess, blaming us for "ruining his life."

Justin didn't know what to believe anymore. And I could hear the weight of it breaking him. Chris was on an emotional rollercoaster, dragging Justin along with him. He manipulated Justin into believing that I should return to the house to discuss the charges, suggesting that perhaps we could reconcile and dismiss the entire "misunderstanding." Justin was aware that we had gone to the police and that CPS was once again involved, now seeking to speak with Chris.

Since I had completely cut off contact with Chris, every time Justin called me, he was instructed to put me on speakerphone. Justin always found subtle ways to warn me that his dad was listening—something I think Chris suspected, but it was the only way.

I could check on Justin and ensure he was okay. Chris knew the detective wanted to meet with him and told Justin he had scheduled an appointment. Unknown calls started coming in. Jeremy and Jess received them too— always silent on the other end.

At first, they were sporadic, but soon they became relentless. No words, just eerie silence. Then Justin put the pieces together. When we switched phone carriers, the company had sent a final bill to our old address. That bill contained our new phone numbers. Chris had them now, and he was the one making the calls— listening, lurking, but never speaking.

On the morning May 22nd, Justin asked if I would be willing to meet with Chris. Chris had convinced him that if we could just talk one last time, we might be able to salvage our marriage and clear up the "lies" being spread about him. At the time, Justin was deeply manipulated. He had spoken to Jess, he knew the truth, but it was almost impossible for him to process the dad he had known with the monster behind the accusations.

Justin truly loved his dad, but I could see the manipulation at play. Chris was pulling him into his web, using guilt and emotional tactics to keep him tangled. I didn't want to meet Chris. I hadn't spoken to him since I left, and every instinct in me screamed that something was off. But years of mental abuse, codependency, and self-doubt had eroded my ability to stand firm.

Guilt weighed heavily on me—the guilt of not being a "good Christian wife." Against my better judgment, I agreed to give him the chance to tell his side of the story. I got dressed and took Jess with me. My plan was simple—keep her in the car so I had an excuse to leave quickly. She had a doctor's appointment at 9:30, and that gave me a built-in exit.

When I arrived, I parked across the street, facing the house. I sat there, staring. The garage—with beautiful brown paint. I remembered how Chris and I had painted it together. The bushes by the porch were the ones my mom and I planted together. The lawn—still perfectly manicured.

It looked so normal. But that's all it was—a house. Never a home. Tears streamed down my face as fear gripped me. Something deep in my gut screamed at me—an alarm blaring inside my head. *STOP. DO NOT ENTER.*

Every instinct told me to turn around, but I silenced them. *It's just a few minutes,* I told myself. *I'll be fine.* Then my phone rang. It was my mom. I hesitated. I knew why she was calling, and I didn't want to answer. She'd ask where I was, and I didn't want to lie—but I also didn't want to tell her the truth.

The phone rang again. With a deep breath, I picked up. "*Chrissie, where are you*?" There it was. Exactly what I didn't want to hear. *"Hi, Mom... why do you want to know?" I tried to sound casual.*

"Chrissie, where are you?" she asked again, her voice more insistent. I swallowed hard. *"Mom, you won't understand, but I'm in front of my house. I'm going inside to talk to Chris. Just for a minute."*

My mom's voice was firm, almost desperate. *"Is Jess with you?" "Yes, she is."* I answered.

"Chrissie, DO NOT go into that house. Please. I've been up since 4 a.m. praying for you and Jess, and I just know something terrible will happen if you go in there." I sighed, frustrated.

"Mom, that's crazy. It'll be fine. It's just a quick conversation. Plus, he said I can pick up Ama's ballerina. My grandmother's dancing ballerina—the only thing I had left from her. It meant everything to me, and I had forgotten it when we left. She didn't budge.

"DO NOT GO IN THAT HOUSE." We went back and forth, her pleading, me insisting. But the longer we argued, the more time passed, and now Jess's doctor's appointment was approaching. I was upset I could've already been done by now. Then, my mom's voice broke.

She was crying. *"Please, Chrissie. I'm begging you."* I couldn't take it. Hearing her cry made something in me snap. *"Okay, Mom. It's fine. I won't go in. I'll come back later... maybe with Jeremy or someone else." "Yes. Please. Just not now"* she said. I sighed. *"Alright. I love you. I'll call you after the appointment."*

While we were at the doctor's appointment, I had no idea that Chris was texting Justin—telling him how much he loved him, how proud he was of him. Justin was waiting at the hub, expecting Chris to arrive so they could take their load to the next destination. But Chris never showed up. Confused and growing anxious, Justin started calling him.

Over and over. No answer.

At the doctor's office, the appointment went as expected. As I stood at the counter, paying, my phone rang. It was Justin's fiancée, Tara.

It was unusual to get a call mid-morning. I was hoping she or my grandson were ok. I picked up. Her voice was shaky. *"Chrissie, Justin told me to call you. You need to go to the house. Chris shot himself. He's gone."* I stood there, the phone pressed against my ear, my mind struggling to catch up. It felt like I had stepped into a dream—one where nothing made sense.

"That's not true," I said automatically. *"He wouldn't do that."* But Tara insisted, her voice breaking. "Chrissie, you need to get to the house. Now."

My first thought was why would Justin put Tara in a position to lie to me like that? Was his dad making him go crazy as well? I didn't have time to process—I just got in the car and drove. My mind raced with disbelief.

There's no way he actually did this. This has to be some kind of sick joke. If this is just a ploy to get me to come back and talk to him, he's taken it way too far. A whirlwind of what ifs consumed me. Should I have stayed? Should I have gone this morning? Should I have answered his calls? Should I have believed him when he said we could get counseling and be a happy family again? Then, a sudden realization hit me like a jolt- If this is true, we need prayer.

I grabbed my phone and called my friend Patty from back home. My voice trembled as I told her what had happened, that Justin was already at the house. Without hesitation, Patty said, *"I'll gather a group of intercessors— we'll start praying for Justin and the entire family right now."* I kept driving, my hands gripping the wheel as my heart pounded in my chest.

As I reached the corner of my block, I instinctively slowed down. From that moment on, everything felt like it was moving in slow motion. Turning onto my street, my breath caught in my throat. Yellow tape stretched across the entire property, sealing off all four corners.

The road was blocked. Flashing lights reflected off the pavement —police cars, a firetruck, an ambulance.

A sea of people gathered outside, hushed voices murmuring in little clusters. Neighbors stood in groups, whispering, pointing toward the house. I followed their gaze, but my mind refused to process what they were seeing. It felt surreal, like I had stepped into someone else's nightmare.

I parked my car and slowly got out of it. My gaze shifted in the direction of a young man screaming in the front yard. He was screaming at the top of his lungs, *"What took you so long", you should have come sooner"*. His screams made the hair on my arms stand up. All I could see was a cloud. Like I was walking but I couldn't feel my feet.

The young man screaming was my son Justin. He had come to the house to check on Chris when he never arrived at the hub. He found him. He had gone into the house and seen the incident possibly minutes after it happened. I wanted to run to him, but I couldn't make my legs move.

The air felt heavy. As I turned, I saw everyone—talking, staring, their eyes fixed on me. Justin's screams were unrelenting. He was covered in blood—his hands, his shirt, his face. The sight of him, the sound of his agony, paralyzed me. I had never heard screams like that before—deep, gut-wrenching - the kind that made the hairs on my arms stand on end.

I, on the other hand, was arguing with Tara. As if making her the target of my anger was going to subside the chaos all around us. She didn't deserve that, and I don't make excuses for my behavior. Nothing here was her fault, yet there I was, yelling when I should have been holding my son, his future wife and my grandson, letting them know it was going to be ok.

Justin's voice suddenly shattered through it all. "Stop fighting!" he yelled at us. The screaming had stopped and just like that, everything fell silent.

It was as if the whole world had paused. To my right, a man in a black suit approached me. His lips moved, but I couldn't hear a single word. I leaned in, straining to understand, but his voice was lost in the thick, suffocating air. Later, I would learn he was from the Episcopal church that Tara's family attended—but in that moment, all I could think was, why is he here?

I moved through the crowd, my eyes moving from face to face, to the yellow tape, to the flashing lights. Then, I saw it—the hearse. Why is there a hearse here? Everything around me felt like it was moving in slow motion. My feet carried me toward the front door, but each time I tried to step onto the porch, an officer blocked my path. Frantic, I turned to them. "What happened?" I demanded. "Is he okay?" My voice wavered as I searched their faces for any sign of hope.

"Isn't someone going to help him?" My voice cracked. *"Is this some kind of joke?" "Why am I allowed not to go inside?"* A voice behind me cut through the chaos. *"She's his wife—close the front door."* Before the officer could shut it, my eyes locked onto the hallway. There, between the kitchen and the living room, I saw his legs—still, unmoving.

He was wearing his blue shorts. Feeling that lump in my throat I could see he wasn't moving. Then—slam. The door shut in my face. *"Mrs. Moore, you cannot go inside. You cannot go inside."* My mind refused to process what was happening. *Is he really gone?* I couldn't get it to make sense.

I turned and walked towards the street, feeling the heavy weight of what I just saw. The morning sun burned hot against my skin. I sat on the asphalt, staring blankly at the crowd. *"Why do they keep staring at me?"* I wanted to tell them to leave but it's almost like they enjoyed watching other people's pain.

After a few moments, I laid back on the asphalt with my eyes looking at the sky. Some clouds drifted quickly, while others lingered as if they too, were unsure where to go. A light breeze skimmed across my forehead, but the heat from the pavement radiated up my back. Then, I felt someone lie down beside me. It was Jess. She had been asking everyone the same question—"Is someone going to help my dad?"

In the distance, Justin's screams had softened into heavy, broken sobs. His pain echoed around me, but I couldn't move. I wanted to go to him, to hold him, but I was frozen in place. I tried to speak—tried to force out any words—but nothing came.

My mouth was dry, my throat tight. I couldn't even swallow. I closed my eyes, just for a moment. Is this real? Or am I trapped in some horrible nightmare? I kept them shut, willing everything to disappear—to wake up and find none of this had happened. But when I opened them again, reality was still there.

I took a slow, shaky breath. The scent of hot asphalt filled my nose. The dampness of freshly watered grass drifted from the neighbor's yard. The rhythmic *click-click* of the sprinkler echoed in the quiet, swinging back and forth, back and forth. Footsteps moved along the sidewalk, slow and aimless.

Shadows passed over me—figures moving around, watching, whispering—yet no one spoke to me. I lay there in complete disbelief, Jess still beside me. Then, through the haze of my grief, I heard a voice—low, heavy, eerie and familiar.

It was the same voice I heard when I was 16 and contemplated taking my own life due to the violence in my home. It wasn't loud, yet it carried a weighted presence that pressed into me. *"Will you still serve God now?"* I froze. Had I imagined it? Or is someone standing behind me? I didn't answer. Then I heard it again. *"Will you still serve God now?"*

The second time I heard it, it was as if the sun had been swallowed by a thick, gray cloud. The air around me grew heavy, like the sky before a storm. A darkness crept in, pulling me toward an abyss of despair. I could feel myself slipping—I knew this darkness too well. This darkness wasn't new—it was an old, relentless shadow of Depression that stood at my door, beckoning me back into the abyss I battled every single day to escape. It reached for me, pulling, tempting me to surrender to its familiar grip.

I could feel myself slipping as if I had fallen into a deep dark hole. But then— something deep within me stirred. My body was weak, my heart shattered into a million pieces, and the weight of what lay ahead threatened to crush me.

Yet, somehow, I found the strength to get up. My legs trembled beneath me, but I planted my feet, refusing to fall. And with every last ounce of strength in me, I spoke out loud. "*Yes. I will still serve my God, even now.*"

Just as I stood up, a woman approached me. "*Are you Mrs. Moore?" "Yes,*" I barely managed to whisper. *"I need to ask you a few questions, if you have a moment."* I nodded, though I felt completely disconnected, as if I were floating outside my own body.

I knew she was speaking to me, but I wasn't sure I'd even be able to process her words. *"Were you supposed to be here today?" she asked.* Her question didn't make sense. I must have looked confused because she clarified, "*Were you supposed to come over and see Mr. Moore today?"* I hesitated, my mind struggling to find clarity. "*I... I don't know. I can't remember. I think so.*"

The fog in my head felt impossible to clear, but then, like a switch flipping, it all came back to me. "*Oh. Yes. He had asked my son if I could come by to talk—try to work things out. I was also going to pick up my grandmother's ballerina, a gift she had left to me when she passed away. He promised to give it to me because he knew how much it meant.*"

The detective's eyes softened with something like sorrow, but also certainty. *"Mrs. Moore I've been doing this a long time, and I know ," she said gently, "this may sound strange, but I believe your husband was planning to kill you, your daughter, and then himself."*

I stood there, motionless. No expression.

I looked at her, but the words wouldn't come. She could

see it—shock was written all over my face. *"He would never do that,"* I finally whispered. *"I know he had issues, but he would never try to kill me."* The detective reached for my hand, her grip firm yet gentle. *"Mrs. Moore," she said carefully, "we recovered a fully loaded mag in the gun.*

He was going to kill you both, then himself—especially with the open CPS case against him. He knew he was facing a long time in prison." I felt the ground shift beneath me. My legs wobbled, and a wave of dizziness hit me.

"Mrs. Moore," she continued, *"someone was really looking out for you and your daughter today."* My body gave in, and I sank onto the sidewalk.

The world around me felt distant. Brandy knelt beside me. "*I'm going to pick up Jeremy*," she said softly. "*I'll also get word to Josh since he's nearby at college."* I heard her.

I knew what she was saying. But I was still trapped in disbelief, frozen in a reality I wasn't ready to accept. I picked up the phone and called my mom. The moment she answered, I broke down, sobbing so hard I could barely form words. But somehow, through the gasps and tears, I managed to say, "C*hris is dead... he shot himself in the chest.*"

I realized that until that moment, I hadn't said it out loud. I couldn't accept what he had done. He took his life to avoid the consequences, and now, I am left with all the broken pieces. Her voice, steady and soothing, cut through my pain. Even though she was 500 miles away, just hearing her made me feel safe. Over and over, she kept saying, "*Thank God you're both okay. Thank God.*"

I survived that day because my mom listened to the voice of God, urging her to wake up at 4 a.m. and pray for me and Jess. She had no idea what was coming, but later, she told me she had woken up wailing—mourning, as if she had already lost us.

She woke up George (my stepdad) and they both interceded for us, and God heard their petitions. I lived that day because

God wasn't finished with me. I lived that day, even though it was meant for me to die. Later, I learned that when Justin found Chris, he tried desperately to help him, but he realized there was nothing he could do, because he was already gone. Grief consumed him.

In that moment of overwhelming pain, he raised the gun to his own head. But then, a thought stopped him—Brayden. His two-year-old son (my grandson) The image of Brayden growing up without a father pulled him back from the edge. I truly believe God's hand was over all of us that day. Eventually, Jeremy and Josh arrived at the house. Our family was shattered.

None of us got the chance to say goodbye. None of us got to release the weight of what we had carried of the pain he inflicted on all of us, especially for what he had done to Jess.

The wounds he had left in all of us; the approval we never got, and the tainted love he shared only left us with more questions than answers. And me? I never got to say all the things I had buried deep inside my heart for years. Had this happened because I wanted him dead? Did I want this whole thing to play out?

Ironically even when the abuser is no longer in your life, you tend to STILL blame yourself for the pain they went through even though the pain they inflicted was so much worse.

The next day felt like waking up from a nightmare—only it wasn't a dream. It was real. I lay in bed, wishing it weren't true, but the hardest part was still ahead of me: picking up the pieces. Brandy gently reminded me that I needed to start planning the memorial service. *Memorial service?*

The thought hadn't even crossed my mind. Not only had he left without apologies or closure, but now I was the one who had to arrange his final goodbye. In my heart, I didn't want to do it—but I knew I had to. I wanted to honor him, to see this through with strength.

Several days passed as I struggled to find the right words, piecing together a PowerPoint of our family's memories—vacations, outings, moments frozen in time. Each time I played it back, I had to hold myself together.

My eyes were swollen from exhaustion, my body felt unbearably heavy, but I pushed forward.

Then came the phone calls. His family. My family. One by one, I explained what had happened. Over and over, I repeated the story until I could barely feel anything. The more I spoke, the more numb I became. My heart was hardening, but none of that mattered—I had a job to do. And despite everything, I remained loyal to him, even to the very end.

The day of the service, everything was in place. The music was set, the handouts prepared, the PowerPoint finalized. At the altar, an 11x14 photo of us—taken when we were whole, when we were happy—stood on display.

I had asked my family to arrive early, yet I still found myself sitting on Brandy's denim couch, motionless. Everything that needed to be done was done. Everything was ready. Except me. I had to hold myself together because, even now, I was trying to be the best wife—to the very end. But the more I sat there, the more the anger simmered inside me.

My thoughts spiraled. *I was a good wife. I was loyal. I was kind. I put him first—always. I made sure everything was in order. I prayed for him. I fasted for him. I spoke life into him, even as he drained the life out of me. I loved him unconditionally. I never cared about status, money, titles—none of it mattered to me. I WAS GOOD TO HIM. Even though he broke me.*

I got up and started pacing aimlessly across Brandy's living room. She was talking, trying to explain what needed to be done, but I wasn't listening. Her words faded into the background, drowned out by the storm inside me. Brandy glanced at me, her expression calm and reassuring.

"I'll take Jess. Jeremy will drive you to the church in the truck," she said gently. I muttered under my breath, "*Who cares.*" She didn't flinch. She knew. She saw it coming before I did. Then it erupted. A scream tore through me, raw and coming from a place so deep I hadn't even known it existed.

I screamed again—louder, harsher—until my throat burned.

Then came the cuss words, the rage spilling out in violent waves. I hurled every cuss word I could think of; every ounce of fury I had bottled up inside. I hated him. I hated that he had left me to pick up his mess. I hated that he never got the help he needed. I hated that this could have been prevented. I hated that he took the coward's way out. I hated that I couldn't save him.

I hated that he left me a widow, left his children fatherless. I hated what he did to me. And worst of all? *I never got to tell him.* When the storm finally passed, I collapsed to my knees, my body drained but my lungs finally able to pull in air again.

Brandy knelt beside me, her face warm with understanding. She took my hand and squeezed. *"Jeremy will take you to the service,"* she said softly.

Then she wrapped me in a hug—no judgment, no pity, just love. I wiped my tears, stood up, and got dressed. For the first time in a long time, I had been given permission to *feel.* And for that, I was grateful. I grabbed my purse, walked with Jeremy to the truck, and we drove to the service in silence.

When we arrived, I made my way to the altar and spoke. I have no memory of what I said, but everyone later told me it was beautiful. After the service, a line formed—one by one, people approached, offering their condolences. They shook my hand, spoke softly, and then made their way to the adjoining building where food had been prepared.

Each person told me how strong I was, how brave I had been to stand up there and speak. But I didn't feel strong. I didn't feel brave. In truth, I didn't feel anything at all. I didn't even want to be there. Everyone was trying to be kind, to be respectful, but all I wanted was to run—to escape, to hide in a dark place where no one could find me.

I smiled, nodding at their words, but inside I was screaming. *"If one more person tells me how strong I am, I think I'm going to freaking lose it."* My chest grew tighter with every passing moment. I was shattered, terrified, and completely alone. Because no matter how much pain Chris caused, no matter the damage he left behind—the man I once loved, the man who had been my best friend, was gone. I had no idea how to grieve a man I once loved and a man I came to hate. .

Fighting back tears, I looked up and toward the back of the church. That's when I saw her—a beautiful, short redhead stepping quietly into the line. Red. That was the nickname I had given her years ago. You know those rare friends, the ones you can go years without seeing, but when you do, it's like no time has passed? That was Red. I couldn't believe she was here. She had driven 500 miles just to see me. She smiled. I smiled back.

When it was her turn to give her condolences, she didn't say a word. She just stepped forward and wrapped her arms around me. At first, I tried to pull away. I didn't want to be touched. I didn't want comfort. But she held on. She didn't tell me how strong I was or how brave I'd been. She didn't try to fill the silence with empty words. She just *hugged* me.

And when I finally stopped fighting it, I melted into her arms like a ragdoll. I could *breathe* again. The purest expression of love without saying a single word—is a hug. It was exactly what I needed. And she knew it. She didn't care that there were people still waiting behind her. She didn't let go.

I wept. But this time, it wasn't out of anger. It wasn't from frustration or exhaustion. It was *grief*—real, raw, and unfiltered. The kind I hadn't allowed myself to feel. In that moment, it was as if God Himself was whispering, *"I've got you, Chrissie. I'm holding you up. You don't have to carry this alone".*

After what felt like forever, she finally pulled back, looked me in the eyes, and simply said, *I love you.* And the truth was—I needed to hear it. I had been holding everything together because I *had* to. Because I had no other choice.

When I drove home after the service, I heard a song "Hurt and Healer" played by a Christian Group called "Mercy Me". This song helped me get through the next several years of grieving. The release date of this song was May 22, 2012. Chris shot himself May 22, 2013.

Epilogue
Beauty for Ashes

It has been nearly 12 years since I began walking the path of healing. Each day is still a battle. The first year was a blur, much of it lost to the fog of survival.

I am still healing from the wounds of abuse, still learning what it means to be whole. But through it all, God has placed incredible people in my life—people who have walked beside me, reminding me that I am worthy of love, that I am more than what I endured. Abuse, by definition, is to treat someone with cruelty or violence, especially repeatedly.

That's why healing doesn't happen overnight. It comes in waves—some gentle, some crashing—but always moving forward. One of the hardest things to unlearn is the belief that we still deserve mistreatment. Abuse becomes so ingrained in our identity that we excuse it, even accept it, as normal. Over time, it distorts our understanding of love.

Walking away from an abusive relationship often feels like abandonment. We convince ourselves that we are responsible for them, that if we stay, they will change. We tell ourselves that leaving means we have failed them, that no one else will take care of them. But the truth is, real love doesn't require us to sacrifice ourselves. And healing means learning to choose *us*—even when it feels impossible.

Love does not intentionally hurt someone and then justify the pain with excuses. An abuser will always shift the blame, making the victim feel responsible for their outbursts—convincing them that if they had just done something differently, the abuse wouldn't have happened. And so, we begin to believe we deserve it. And they continue—again and again and again. This is the cycle we learn to live in. We become conditioned to the abuser's emotional highs and lows, so much so that without their chaos, we feel empty, lonely—even missing the very patterns that have harmed us.

Love bombing is intensely showered with affection, gifts, and promises for the future with the abuser so that the victim feels or is made to believe that all this is a sign of true love- Wikipedia paraphrase

You see, you can't abuse a person without having a hook to pull them back in. The abuser must know exactly when to hurt us. Then when we feel like we can't take this abuse any longer, and begin to wonder if there is more to life than this, the love bombing kicks in.

If you are reading this and feel you know exactly what I'm talking about, you could be in an abusive relationship and there is nothing to be ashamed of. God does not want us to live in abuse. He didn't create us for that. He created us to be loved like Christ loves the church. People often say that escaping the abuse is the hardest part—and in many ways, it is. I remember feeling terrified when I finally broke free. But the most difficult part of my healing wasn't leaving—it was untangling myself from the lies that had kept me bound.

It wasn't that I was incapable of loving again. The real battle was overcoming the belief that my abuser was the only one who could ever love me. The mental abuse and manipulation had convinced me that the distorted, conditional love I was given was real. And for so long, I believed I wasn't worthy of anything more.

I even felt like I only wanted men like Chris. This is because I was attracted to trauma or chaos. It's the only thing I've known so it's the very thing that tried to pull me back in.

Resources

Trauma bonds are in fact a real thing. We don't know it because we're in it. But when we come out on the other side, we can see much more clearly. (article from Eliana Galindo-phycologist from Colombia) *https://www.find- a-therapist.com/author/eliana-galindo/*

Trauma bonding often blurs the lines between love and trauma, making it important to understand its dynamics. This bond is characterized by intermittent reinforcement through abuse followed by positive reinforcement, creating a powerful emotional connection. Trauma bonds are often mistaken for love because of the intense attachment that forms despite the presence of harm. Characteristics of Trauma Bonds
The key characteristics of trauma bonds include:

Stages of Trauma Bonding

Characteristics	Description
Dependency	Victims develop a reliance on their abusers for emotional support despite the abusive behavior.
Complex Emotional Attachment	The cycle of abuse and intermittent kindness from the abuser creates a confusing mix of fear, loyalty, and attachment.
Justification of Abuse	Victims may rationalize harmful behaviors as expressions of love or stress.

Trauma bonding typically progresses through stages like:

	Stage	Description
1	Love Bombing	The abuser showers the victim with affection and attention.
2	Trust & Dependency Development	The victim starts to trust and depend on the abuser.
3	Criticism and Abuse	Abusive behavior emerges, and criticism becomes common.
4	Reinforcement	Periods of kindness by the abuser reinforce the bond, creating a confusing cycle of abuse and reward.

All of this to say—there IS hope. There is a way out, and you are not alone. Many of us have survived and lived to tell our stories of triumph. Over the years, I've met countless women from every walk of life—lawyers, nurses, coaches, stay-at-home moms, IT professionals—the list goes on.

And despite our different backgrounds, our stories are the same. We thought it was love. We believed the promises that he would change. But here's my message to you: God is real. He is hope. He created you for a divine purpose, and abuse is not part of His plan for your life. Jesus died to set the captives free, and I was once that captive.

I survived so that I could help others reclaim their voice. For years, mine was silenced—but my prayer is that my story gives you the courage to find yours again. There are resources and organizations in your community ready to help. I know it takes incredible bravery to admit you are being abused—but that courage is beautiful. Find your voice, and when you do, use it to help set others free.

RESOURCES:

One Safe Place-Fort Worth, TX
https://www.onesafeplace.org/

Safe Haven- Fort Worth

https://www.safehaventc.org/

National Domestic Violence Hotline

https://www.thehotline.org

National Sexual Assault Hotline 800-656-HOPE (4673)

https://rainn.org/resources

BIBLIOGROPHY:

- *Played It Well: https://playeditwell.com/6-stages-of-grooming-adults/*
- *Mark Wolynn- https://markwolynn.com/it-didnt-start-with-you/*
- *Psychology Today- https://www.psychologytoday.com/us/blog/head-games/202209/the-5-stages-predatory-sexual-grooming*
- *Trauma Survivors: https://www.fortraumasurvivors.com/post/grooming-in-adult-relationships*
- *Psych Central: https://psychcentral.com/pro/recovery-expert/2018/09/how-victims-are-groomed-by-abusive-predators#1*
- *Cambridge Dictionary*
- *NIV*
- Eliana Galindo-phycologist from Colombia) *https://www.find-a-therapist.com/author/eliana-galindo/*

- Resources:
- One Safe Place-Fort Worth, TX
- https://www.onesafeplace.org/
- Safe Haven- Fort Worth
- https://www.safehaventc.org/
- National Domestic Violence Hotline
- https://www.thehotline.org
- National Sexual Assault Hotline 800-656-HOPE (4673)
- https://rainn.org/resources

About the Author:

Chrissie Moore is the author of *Broken Beautiful*, her debut book dedicated to inspiring women to walk in their triumphs rather than remain trapped in their trauma. She is passionate about empowering women in abusive relationships, showing them that there is a way out—and that a life filled with love, joy, peace, and freedom is possible.

In her spare time, Chrissie enjoys reading, watching movies, and engaging in some "friendly" skeet shooting competitions with her family. For the first time in a long time, she is truly living a life of happiness. She would love to hear from you.

Connect with her on Facebook at *Broken Beautiful Ministries*

Email: *brokenbeautifulministries@gmail.com*

Or visit her website to learn more: http://www.brokenbeautifulministries.org/

Thank you, Brandy.

Your courage is nothing short of beautiful. You opened your home without a second thought to a woman fleeing her abusive husband, along with two kids and three dogs. You didn't hesitate. You didn't back down. You refused to take no for an answer. You gave me a safe space to share my rawest emotions, and instead of judgment, you wrapped me in a hug. You let me be human, and I love you for that.

I can't fathom where my life would be today if you hadn't listened to God's call and helped us find freedom. I love you. I honor you. I'm beyond grateful to call you, my friend.

Everyone needs a Brandy

Made in the USA
Coppell, TX
05 October 2025

60871246R10075